# Through the Fire

Michael Kowch

Copyright © 2018 Michael Kowch
All rights reserved
First Edition

NEWMAN SPRINGS PUBLISHING
320 Broad Street
Red Bank, NJ 07701

First originally published by Newman Springs Publishing 2018

ISBN 978-1-64096-244-6 (Paperback)
ISBN 978-1-64096-245-3 (Digital)

Printed in the United States of America

To the only one I truly love,

                                                YKIIKI

# Foreword by Sandi Athey

Michael's distinctive writing style will instantly transport you to another time and place.

Prepare to travel side by side with him as he shares his perspective on life's unique yet universal lessons. Share in his experience of the full spectrum of human emotion in this candid glimpse into his journey of life, *Through the Fire*.

You will cheer for the sensitive boy becoming a man on his own terms as he courageously embraces his soul in its entirety. Michael's entertaining sense of humor is palpable throughout the peaks and valleys of the story, causing an endearing reaction, making you want to drive to his home and give him a big hug.

I met Michael Kowch in one of my very favorite places … the radio. As a professional intuitive with decades of experience reading people, I've learned that I get my most accurate information by hearing someone's voice. Michael's generosity of spirit and sincere intention to contribute to the goodness of the world was immediately evident when he greeted me on air. We hit it off right away and eventually co-hosted a weekly talk show together. I am honored and proud to have Michael as my colleague, friend, and fellow classmate in this continuing lesson of being human.

Get comfortable on your sofa with a cup of tea or a glass of wine, and experience it for yourself!

# My Reflections

WRITING THIS BOOK HAS BEEN more cathartic than I anticipated. Thankfully, I had the experiences of several nervous breakdowns and the time to reflect upon them. There is also a quiet beauty in realizing that no matter who you think you are, or what you think you have become, or what you think you know, self-realization evolves. An epiphany if you will, where I can be certain the universe has conspired on my behalf and has bestowed upon me its crown of enlightenment. Taking time to be quiet enough to really dive in and search for that pearl of wisdom in the random oyster you choose, is a sublime luxury. I have read *A Course in Miracles,* I enjoy the likes of Marianne Williamson, Wayne Dyer, Zig Ziglar, Tony Robbins, and hell, I even get motivation from the evangelist with the big teeth. Inspiration is everywhere, and I want to drink it up.

After forty-nine years on this earth, I have found a few pearls. I have found a lot of sand as well. Imagine a mason jar filled with pearls, filled to the rim. Is the jar full? No. Now pour sand in and see how it surrounds each pearl. It molds itself, forming a collective purpose. Now is the jar full? No. Now, pour water on top of the sand and the pearls. Notice how the water takes up the last bit of space between the pearls and the sand. Now is the jar full? It is my oyster. It is me. It is all of us. We are a collective entity. Each person, each memory, each thought, each action, affects the collective. More on this thought later. As I have come to know myself deeper, I have reached the conclusion that I have always been different, and I see things uniquely as well.

Until the age of seven, my family lived in a mining town in Manitoba. I do not immediately recall much, except we lived on Steventon Boulevard. We had a collie named Lassie, and Dad worked in the mine digging for nickel and copper. Mother worked as an assistant to the superintendent of schools, and I spent a lot of time with my Baba. Things were pretty normal.

Then, unbeknownst to me, my parents decide to leave Manitoba for the prairies and open a restaurant. Lake Vu Drive Inn, the restaurant, was located on Route 49 in Preeceville, Saskatchewan. Population 1,240, including the squirrels. The restaurant was a drive-in sort where you parked outside along a concrete runway; we took your order and brought your food to your car. I was the only waiter at the time. My seven-year-old ass walked that runway daily after school, and I learned very quickly what being knocked in the face felt like at an early age, literally. Picture it: I, the young boy with innocent intent. Mother had purchased the brownest ensemble available at the time. Brown shirt, brown vest, with orange-and-blue stripes, brown plaid pants, and a brown briefcase. Starting a new school in a town where farming, hunting, fishing, trapping, and skinning animals was the norm, Mother dropped me off. With all the false confidence I could muster, I walked in the first set of doors. I followed the stream of kids that appeared to be my age, rounded the corner and reached for the door knob on the second set of doors when, *wham!* The door knob of the red door smashed into my mouth and knocked out my two front teeth. Stunned by, and not knowing what happened, I received my first taste of blood. I looked down on my brown vest with the orange-and-blue stripes and witnessed what happens when red mixes with orange and blue. Mrs. Pollock attended to me. We went to the bathroom so I could get cleaned up. She was nice: brown, football-shaped hair, brown-rimmed glasses, brown shoes. I was, of course, crying. She wiped my face with cold water and calmly talked me down. I gathered my wits and checked the mirror. I was swollen, tasting blood and missing a couple teeth, but what could I do? I thanked her for her kindness and informed her that I needed to urinate. She pointed me in the direction of a confusing contraption I later learn to be called a urinal.

I had never seen one before. I thought, *Okay* ... I approached the daunting white porcelain stranger. I unbutton my pants, pulled my underwear down, and I proceeded to sit down on the little drain. Mid-stream, Mrs. Pollock swiftly rushed over to inform me of the error of my way, promptly provided me with the appropriate protocol of urinal usage, and I corrected myself thusly. That was the first day of my second year of elementary school.

Learned a lot.

I never again used the wrong door. I later realized they were clearly marked, and I never again sat to pee in the urinal. My academic career in a town of foreign concepts was orthodox for the region. For some reason, I really did think that I was right and everyone else was different. *Why aren't these people thinking as I do?* This would take some work on my part.

I realized I was gay by the age of seven, but I did not "really" know what "fag" meant until the age of eight. I did not know I needed to hide it. By the time I realized I needed to hide the fact that I liked boys, (men, to be precise), it was too late. Everyone knew. There was only one "other" in the entire school that was great at art, had a great voice, made his own clothing, and hung out with the girls. I studied him. Also, saw him fend off four others. Girl could handle herself. Danny was his name. He attended home economics, sewed his own clothes, and was friends with all the best-looking girls in the school. In a way, I think that he was some sort of threat to the other boys dressed in plaid and dirty work boots. Danny and I had last period off during Tuesdays. We were in the library. Keith Antonichuck and Kevin Belysky were literally firing spit balls at the back of Danny's head. Watching the whole event unfold was troubling yet, I couldn't turn away. After nearly four minutes of this barbaric behavior, and after being shushed by Mrs. Tulick who instructed them to keep down the giggling, Danny calmly gathered his books and left the library. Keith and Kevin followed Danny out into the hallway. As Danny was putting his books in his locker, the two assholes started to push him around a little, mimicking a pinball in a machine. Verbal taunting, although not at all clever, was still cutting and escalating the impromptu gathering. Danny closed his locker and replaced the combination lock. He took off his coat, removed his silver hoop earrings and tossed them on the coat on the floor. Watching from behind the library door, I don't remember him saying a word. Danny bent down to tie his shoe while still being demeaned verbally. As he stood up, he struck Kevin with a right hook to the chin, causing Kevin to hit the stained orange carpet. This took Keith by surprise. While Keith was looking at Kevin on the floor, Danny wound up his right leg, and planted a swift kick to Keith's tiny, pigeon-sized ball sac. (We showered together after gym class and I couldn't understand where the hell he found his confidence while having such a tiny penis.) Danny picked up his earrings and placed them in the pocket of his wool vest. He had made an *A* on it in our home economics class. Threw his jacket over his left shoulder and walked out the door. I watched them writhe and slowly gather themselves while giggling very hard under my breath. That's the kind of fag I wanted to be.

I was the class treasurer, yearbook editor, had a weekly column in the local paper, was campaign manager for the Winter Queen Pageant. The quote under my high school picture in the category Theme Song was Working for the Weekend.

I was that person.

For those of you who were raised in the family restaurant business arena, I applaud you. Thankfully, my ambition is a pearl from my parents. They honestly molded my psyche with how hard you have to work to get a dollar. Mom developed a successful and working business model and even gave back to the community. She, as a career woman, reached out to the high school, recruited some of the more intellectual others to give them much valued work experience; they had something to put on their resumé before they were thrown to the wolves. Dad decided to expand and added a sit-down café that seated thirty people minimum. The fresh produce even came from our gardens. Thinking back, we were farm to table.

I worked every day. I was line cook by the age of fifteen. The gals and I worked well together. They knew how to handle a rush hour with efficiency and charm. Here's another good reference to forest thinkers versus tree thinkers. Let's say you get ten tables at once that walk in or pull up. You have ten orders in front of you as a cook. Now, do you do one order at a time, or do you count how many burger patties you need to start, how many orders of fries to drop, a few orders of onion rings, maybe a few hot dogs as well. Now, all is cooking and you have time to ready the buns, pull the needed sides together, and eventually finish ten orders in the time it would have taken you to do one. That's the way I tend to think. I had two favorite things to do. When the restaurant closed, we had to finish up dishes, fill the condiments for the morning shift, sweep the floors, pick up the trash outside, and hopefully get out of there in about an hour. There was a window above the sink in the kitchen. Remember, we were five miles out of town, and when night fell, the stillness coupled with the darkness could be a little creepy. Music would be playing on the radio but I learned, that even when you're busting a move to Duran Duran, a couple loud bangs on the window that forces you to look up and see a face looking back at you, will always scare the crap out of you. My favorite trick was while I was counting cash and balancing the nights take, I would remind one of the gals to lock the bathrooms. The bathrooms were not inside the restaurant; they were around the building so you had to get up from your inside table, go outside, and walk around the corner to process the necessary void. I would watch as they finished whatever they were doing, then run outside to the bathroom, quickly run cold water over my hands and wait. You had to open the door, then reach around to lock the door from the inside. As the gal reached around the dark, square room, my cold, wet hands would grab theirs. Screaming, profanities, and an elevated heart rate was always fun to witness. It never got old, and they fell for it every time.

 My desires were fickle at best. When I watched *The Paper Chase*, I wanted to be a lawyer. When I watched *Fame*, I would want to perform. When I would watch *C.H.I.P.S*, I would think, "Boy, the blond one is cute!" Consequently, I grew to loathe the restaurant. There was no time for after-school activities. I had to be ready for the dinner rush each day. I worked weekends, emptied grease traps, cleaned the ice-cream machine, which was a real pain in the ass. Power wash the vent screens, and the stainless-steel backsplash, empty the bug zapper, all the glory jobs. Washed and waxed floors every Sunday morning, and while the floors were drying, worked meal-prep for the Sunday buffet, when people piled food on plate after plate, mimicking a ravenous bear preparing for winter. My senior year, I reached a critical point and begged Mother to let me take an after-school job at the local clothing store instead of spending all my time in the restaurant. She acquiesced. My ulterior motive was being able to drive to school, rather than taking the school bus. My daily life then: Up at six to walk over (our home was two hundred feet away from the restaurant), start the fryers, the flat top grill, and start the soup du jour. Once things were in order, Dad's 1974 rust suffused Chevy king cab work truck with an enormous toolbox was mine, and it ran beautifully. I had to be in class by 8:45 a.m., but when the noon bell rang, I would quickly drive the five minutes back home to work the lunch shift. As the lunch shift died down, I would run to the house and change into my clothing-store-after-school clothes. Often, an ensemble including a pair of wool slacks, shirt, paisley patterned vest, and tie, and drove back for afternoon classes.

(Remember, most kids my age were of the agricultural background. So, anything outside of oil-and-mud-stained jeans and a bunny hug was out of the norm. Afternoon ridicule seemed as much of the schedule as any other event.) Classes ended at 3:45 p.m., and I would hurry to Athletes Anonymous. It was a store specializing in shotguns, fishing lures, hunting traps, and, under the same roof, clothing for the entire family with the latest styles of running shoes, and local artisan jewelry. Hell, they even sold pantyhose, and why that stands out is beyond my understanding. The store would close at six, and I would drive back for the dinner crowd rush. This usually died out by eight-ish, the theatre pulled the crowds from their evening consumption indulgences regularly. We would clean up; I would start homework in anticipation for the after-theatre crowd. We generally would close at 10:00 p.m. Leaving time to clean up, walk home to finish homework, maybe watch a bit of television, and hit the sack to ready myself for Groundhog Day to start again promptly at 6:00 a.m. the next morning. I was sixteen when I really got my first dose of understanding. I awoke one Friday morning, ready for the day. As I stumbled to the bathroom in a sleepy stupor, I noticed mom's feet sticking out from the orange chair. Turning the corner, I noticed her on the floor on her side and blue in color, gasping for air. Her speech was faint and her eyes weren't really focusing. Where was Dad? I look out the window and see his work van and truck so he must be at the restaurant. I woke up my sister and brought her out to mother. Told her I was going to look for Dad. I was thinking I would check there first and call the ambulance from the restaurant. Dad is not there; I make the call. I run back the thirty feet to the house, open the door, and see my sister crying, (she must have been eight years old at the time), Mother still in the same position, but clearly weaker and more purple. I move mother on her back and we held her head as the ambulance arrived. The paramedics came in and assessed the situation, a gurney was brought in, and right behind it was Dad, covered in soil. Apparently, he was down in the garden, pulling potatoes for the day. Oblivious to what was going on, his weak attempt at concern was more than evident. He did not seem phased one bit. Mother is loaded into the noisy van. Dad took my sister, and I went to the hospital with Mother in the ambulance.

She was diagnosed with a severe case of pneumonia and was rushed to Regina. Three hours away, it was the closest civilization with adequate medical facilities, and it was there she spent a month recovering. At sixteen, I found myself balancing restaurant management, tending to my studies, and keeping up with my myriad of responsibilities. My Baba came to live with us for the month mother was gone and was witness to what I overlooked with regard to my father's inability to handle anything emotionally stressful. He was always working a job out of town. Except to eat or criticize, he rarely set foot in the restaurant. Both talents grew old incredibly quickly, and I remember being pushed past my vocal inhibitions by the criticism late one night. How does a sixteen-year-old explain they're worn out, they are tired, they are frustrated, and they are exhausted? Was he ever going to contribute on the home-front? He recommended that I get some sleep. Once Mom had returned from the hospital, she and Dad decided to lease the restaurant to a couple from the big city. After years around the greasy air, coupled with smoking three to four packs of Benson and Hedges 100s for many years, her lungs were not strong enough. She did quit smoking, but it took years for her to heal. The logical move was to lease the space to another. The customers wouldn't care much as long as the quality of the food remained the same.

Kenny was a hairdresser, much like my great-grandfather and grandmother, or Baba as I called her. Kenny's lover, Dan, looked like Tom Selleck with a hair lip, yet was still very attractive. They lived in a camper my father rented to them. Conveniently enough, during my senior exams, I used the camper to concentrate on studying as well. One afternoon, Dan came into the camper while I was studying and took a shower ...

As I mentioned, I knew I was gay early in life, and I somehow managed to coerce a few family members into exploration with me. By eighteen, I had a few memorable experiences with men. Dan was certainly one to remember. However, the town was small and word traveled fast. The town's weekly rag featured stories of who visited whom over the weekend, and pictures of Mrs. Broadziak hanging out her laundry during the freezing cold. Hard-hitting news. Father had learned of a rumor in our mill of a town ... I had relations with Dan, the rumor told. So, during dinner one night, he asked me outright if I was gay. Mother flew into a rage, propelling the silk flower arrangement at his head, sobbing in motherly defiance and protection, wondering what she did wrong to raise her son to be gay. I gave credence to the rumor mill and admitted to my indiscretion, feeling relieved that I no longer need pretend. I did so very selfishly knowing that my days in the town were numbered, and I no longer had to be anything other than who I was. Somehow, I unconsciously assumed that everyone did the same. The truth shall set you free. Looking back, everyone had secrets, and each wore the mask they needed in order to live their lives with the least resistance. Later on, I would learn of my mother's deception, and where I get my ability to manipulate a situation. A valuable tool, but best used with good intention. Family history would reveal that Mom and Dad got married shotgun style, she with child. In reality, Mother was not pregnant when she married Father. A sort of entrapment, if you will. She feigned a miscarriage once the ring was on her finger, and I arrived five years later to surprise everyone.

The irony, in retrospect, is that it took more energy to be false than to be authentic. The energy used to fuel our collective facades could light the town.

I could not wait to get out of that town. I graduated high school on a Friday and left the following Sunday. Three-and-a-half hours away from the torment and ridicule I was getting started in the big city to attend Richard's Beauty School in Regina. Regardless of the reputation I had, I could start all over again. This was a whole new start, the grain of sand for a new pearl.

However smart I thought I was in that little ensnaring town, moving to the big city revealed a plethora of hidden knowledge and emotional cacophony abounded. I was nervous, I was happy, I was scared, and I was excited. Nervous, because what I knew would be challenged. It was easy to meander through my home town, very little ever changed; common variables each day offering predictability. Happy, because I was free to leave, run away, and never look back. Scared, because of the known unknowns I was sure to encounter. Excited, because it was time to see if who I really was, was the person I thought I wanted to be. All at once and not soon enough.

I had no clear starting point past post-graduation evacuation. I called on my Aunt Anna to help find a place for me and my high school friend, now new roommates. She picked an apartment on the extreme north side of town, inconceivably far away from the school I was attending. It took two transfers to get downtown and an hour on the bus, one way. Winter in Saskatchewan. The last winter I endured eleven consecutive days of minus 77 degrees Celsius and over eighteen feet of snow. The busses kept running, people never missed a day of work. Before it was over, I would find an apartment four minutes away on foot. I was armed with what my parents had put away for my education, all twelve hundred dollars, and a sizeable student loan. I excelled at my classes and quickly became the student that could always go the extra mile for the faculty and my peers. I smoked my first joint at eighteen and was never a stranger to a good cocktail.

I was that person now.

The gay life in Regina was evident, a college city with a strong student body involved in the arts. Weekends usually involved a drive to The McKim, an artists' haven. Singers, painters, budding philosophers, musicians feely roamed the stairwell Sunday mornings. All the front doors were open, the smell of artisan coffee brewing, and hash oil danced about, giving you the much-appreciated contact high. I thought it was all so charming. I met my first boyfriend, Christopher, in a gay bar in Saskatoon, sister city three hours away. He was a computer engineer with a minor in political science. He was fascinating to talk with and possessed a dry sense of humor. He was philosophical, extremely well read, and was friends with a group of like-minded people.

Chris had his good points. However, after only eight years, it came to light that he had terrible hygiene, rolled his own cigarettes out of a pack of Old Drum tobacco, which left his first two fingers as tar stained as his two front teeth. He had a cat named Ziggy, fat and white, with two different-colored eyes who would never shit in the litter tray/box, presumably because the overwhelming ammonia smell from weeks of defecation and urination formed an invisible barrier against any entry. His mother thought she was *fabulous* and continually worked to prove it to you. I ended the romance when I learned of a hand-written letter from Chris to a young man named Troy, a dental student who we had be-friended. The letter explained that Chris felt some "magic" when their feet brushed together at a recent dinner party. Troy called me and told me of the love letter immediately. We laughed, then I hopped into Chris's BMW and drove three-and-a-half hours with the intention of bedding Troy to get back at Chris. Adolescent? Indeed. Fun? Indeed. The fun and bedding ended when a local officer came calling upon the occupants of Troy's place. Chris had reported the car stolen. I had to explain myself to the nice police officer and hightail it back to face Chris. Blowout.

Yelling.

Tears. Queers can be so dramatic. Chris moved out later that night. With that dramatic episode behind me, it left me time to explore where this hair thing was taking me. I volunteered at the local theatre, did hair for commercials, fashion shows, and charity events. I continued my education with a hair product company. Quickly becoming a top trainer and educator doing main stage work at industry functions for crowds of thousands. Travel took over my non-salon days, and for four years, I traveled more than thirty weekends out of the year.

I eventually grew bored with hair …

I partnered with a local modeling agency, rented a small workplace, and promoted young, aspiring models to the international market. I had two gals who went on to have a pretty decent career, and I learned a lot about the entertainment market. Some extremely good, some extremely bad.

Things were looking good for me. My appointment book was full of clients at the salon, my gals were doing well in Tokyo and New York, and I was actually getting paid to do stage hair instead of countless hours of pro bono work. I was traveling doing training for Paul Mitchell Systems as well, and I was still modestly bored. In Saskatchewan, the fashion is almost two years behind the rest of the world, if not more. The trends and noteworthy styles were coming out of Toronto and Vancouver, two cities that could not be farther apart. In an endeavor to extend all horizons, again partnering with the modeling school that I rented work space from, I put it to the team one night after a bottle of Irish whiskey that we bring the coastal fashion market to our little city. They had the models. I had the access to actors, dancers, musicians. I had more than enough staff to handle the hair and makeup needs. I had recently bought the salon where I was working. The previous owner and one of my mentors retired, knee problems of all things. Along with the purchase of the salon, came stock in the school I attended, if I was willing to teach a couple classes a week. A chance that I leapt on. Our purpose was to locate new and upcoming designers from all arenas in Canada for one extravagant showcase. A coming-out party of sorts, no pun intended. Clothing would be shipped to a central location; we had over sixty models to show over 250 pieces over a ninety-minute show. We would commission someone to write original music keeping with the mood of clothing lineup. It would be held in the grand ballroom of the Hotel Saskatchewan, the queen's royal headquarters when she came to town. Tickets were one hundred dollars per person; allowing access to cocktails and light fare, mingling opportunities with the designers in attendance, free champagne, and a s.w.a.g. bag, supplied by the lovely people of Neutrogena. One of my runway gals, Jodi, and I were recently at Ford Model Agency in New York chatting with Katie Ford herself about how Jodi's legs were simply two inches too short, but still had "such a stunning face," we decided on a spokes model. Lauren Hutton was available for fifteen grand, half up front, half upon completion. I had followed her for years and knew a bit of her backstory. What could go wrong, right? The response was amazing. Almost all the designers we approached with the idea wanted to jump on board. Clothing arrived by larger and larger parcels, cataloguing would soon prove to be a challenge. We were training the models for the standard walk, reviewing hours of footage, and walking till their once-beautiful toes looked like the gnarled complements of a prima ballerina. Hair and makeup went over our contributors "look books" to ensure that the essence of every look was appropriately exhibited. Posters were printed, radio spots were dubbed, television spots were recorded, newspaper interviews were given, and personal and professional networks were tapped to reach all those involved and interested. Ticket sales were slow, but most purchases were usually made the night before an event that did not include a fiddle or a harmonica.

 We seemed to have all working parts in place. The event was called Concept Nouveau, or New Concept. It was to be held on October 31, Halloween night. Yes, we did think of having costumes included. However, with the designs we were showing, no one would know who was in a costume and who was not. Lauren was to arrive the night before, get settled, and prep all day for the evening event. I was bursting with anticipation. I rose sluggish, the morning of our last day of preparations, tumbled out of bed and stumbled toward the kitchen. I did not pour myself a cup of caffeinated ambition immediately; my bladder was guiding the autopilot this morning. I proceeded to the bathroom. I loved my bathroom. Picture an oversized claw-foot tub, Tiffany's inspired subway tile to the ceiling, and a glorious stained-glass window granting the barest modesties. While relieving myself of my aqueous retentions, I looked out of the top of the window, which was clear and saw the snow gently falling against a winter morning sky. My mission complete, I found my way to the kitchen to start coffee and headed out for my morning cigarette on the deck. I opened up the decking door to discover that roughly three feet of white powder had already settled, and it was only 8:00 a.m. Panic started resonating and grew in amplitude. I needed meteorological assurances from the news cast on good ole CBC. Fuck me, the only thing I gave no heed was the one thing I had no control over. Screw the coffee. I threw myself together and headed to the Hotel Saskatchewan. My partners' faces met me looking as white as the snow on the ground. We would learn that a blizzard was certainly not only here, but would increase in intensity roughly the same time Lauren's flight was due to land. Scramble sequence initiated. If she did not land, we had no MC. We had sold only 20 percent of the tickets. Only the die-hards would show up in this weather and now the remaining tickets that we intended to push on the radio during the day would surely not move. All the food was ready to serve the five hundred people we were expecting, but if only forty people showed up, we still had food for five hundred. The Royal Suite, which goes for twelve hundred dollars a night, would go empty. The chances of all the models showing up was narrow. Our beautiful castle of cards was going to fall. Painfully.

What could we do to thwart Mother Nature's icy condemnation?

Five of us hit the streets close to the hotel and surrounding businesses and gratuitously giving the tickets away with the hope that at least we would have a full audience when the press was in active coverage of the event. They would not know otherwise. On the phone we were confirming that all was kosher at the airport. Delays, but no cancellations. We powered through the radio spots, which was more satisfying than anticipated. In a last-ditch effort to garner support and turn-out during an interview, I made an executive decision to give a portion of the proceeds to the provincial AIDS research program. This proved to be the more influential tact in the end, but we had to make it out of expenses and into actual proceeds first. Baby steps ...

The underlying challenge of the day was keeping my ensuing bowel-liquifying panic in check to remain on task with our damage control blitz. Silent prayer was not going to be enough. Truth be told, I had one of those sneezing jags during my anal-retentive quest for control. A little something came out on sneeze number four, I wasn't really sure from which end, but I had no time to worry about that.

However, sometimes it does. Lauren's plane landed with a one-hour delay, and she arrived safely with her tall, manly-looking female bodyguard. She graced the steps to the hotel, wearing a black sable fur and matching fur hat. With the hotel manager alongside us, we greeted her, exchanged the appropriate curbside pleasantries, and the group VIP'd her to her suite upstairs.

Honestly, it was like a scene in the movies. I love a good movie moment in real life.

The manager, Lenny, showcased the suite for event's elite, and parroted the pertinent information needed to make her stay most enjoyable. Lenny waved his good-bye, and through the red-and-gold brocade double doors leading to the hallway, took his leave.

With Lenny's act complete, Lauren turned to us. She yanked her fur cap off, and revealed her fine, wavy, blonde hair so full of static there was an angelic halo of individual strands as the hall light broke through the supernatural display. She addressed the event staff, "I need a Scotch, who wants one?" She kicked off her black, velvet Ralph Lauren flats and unbuttoned her floor-length black, sable fur coat, she floated to the corner bar barely pausing to drop her fur on the gold-gilded captain's chair at the end of the banquet table. *This gay man was getting lady wood.* We went over the itinerary for the event day, while ice cubes clinked in our Waterford highball glasses. We all giggled from time to time, went over her needs and wants, and bid each other good night. I was very professional; I think I was twenty-four. I walked over to the Hotel Saskatchewan to start our day the next morning. Show Day. I was to do Lauren's hair, her nails were to be done, then on to lunch, and then press for CBC, MuchMusic, CICC, CTV, NBC with a couple radio remotes live from the hotel. The snow seemed at bay, but she can be a finicky bitch when she wants. Models, hair, and makeup were arriving and setting up. I thought, *Holy shit, we may pull this thing off.* I knock on Lauren's door. In my mind, I am thinking, *Are we now on a first name basis after our little Scotch bonding session, or do I call her Ms. Hutton? Am I wearing too much cologne? Did I put on deodorant today? Why cannot I stop sweating?* I remained stoic, the picture of professional, while clutching my bag of hair trickery. She opens the door and sings, "Mikey! Join me for a pancake?" She led me to the large, mahogany, hand-carved dining table to break our fasts. Attired in a simple white T-shirt, ripped jeans, touted bare feet, shoulders covered by miles of sable, she sat cross-legged and ate her pancake with her hand. I shit you not, it was a pure Julia Roberts moment from *Pretty Woman*, before *Pretty Woman* was even a storyline. We did her hair sitting on the marble floor that the Queen of England herself has literally had *Reflections from the Throne*. She told me about Charleston, the infamous gap in her teeth, a couple of stories about Eileen Ford and the model house, being kissed by Richard Gere, and her Revlon contract. I was fascinated, star struck. I am sure saliva dripped as I drank in all I could. I felt we had a connection ... then, *snap!* I realized I was talking to one of the industry's most iconic individuals, and she was going to MC a show that I produced. Holy shit balls, I had better pull it together. My intestines began the butter-churn once again, with vigor.

There are moments in my career that I look back on and seriously consider all things that were in motion. I cannot believe where I was or what I was doing, but I was doing it. I was actually doing it.

These pearls are now evident in many of my experiences. My time with Lauren Hutton is certainly in the bounds of my jar of pearls.

On with Concept Nouveau!

Happy hour was at 7:00 p.m.; the show started at 8:00 p.m. People showed up, but filled a thin fifth of the venue seats. On-the-fly problem solving. We lumped them all together to avoid a sparse showing in news footage. The media outlets buzzed, and the original score written by the ever talented, and soon to be revealed ass hat, Shawn Greenshields. *His last name always reminded me of a tacky, name-branded, biodegradable panty-liner.* Cue the lights ...

The house lights down, fade to black, and cue music …
Bring up the fronts in eight. S-l-o-w-w-w-w-l-y.
"Mark, send out Meagan on the last beat after eight."
"Have a *great* show everyone."

Let's do this! That is always the time when my heart races, and I get that feeling. The show went off very well, few blunders, but only those in the know would notice. The crowds graciously offered their congratulations on a job well done, and loitered in the hopes of stealing a picture with Lauren. She was a marvelous! The evening reluctantly simmered down. We left the hotel staff to clean, and we all went our separate ways after patting ourselves on our backs. I was exhausted, but in such a good, whole, and complete way, it was a welcomed guest. Later, I would learn that Lauren stole herself away from her bodyguard and made her way to The Georgia. It was a rough and tough bar with bad live music and dirty glasses to say the very least. Bikers, parolees, and those with loose morals made up the scene. She got back to the hotel around 4:00 a.m.

We all gathered the next morning at 10:00 a.m. to go over the results. Sales, contracts, and all the minutiae involved for our meeting with Lauren at 11:00 a.m. While waiting, I learn that we had lost money on the show and would certainly end up in the red on this one.

I felt a tap on my shoulder and looked up and right into Lauren's nostrils. "I need your help for a minute," she says. She led me to the bathroom in her suite and pointed toward the baroque, hand-laid porcelain sink. There, on top of the beautifully handcrafted work of art, is a four-inch-long stain of what can only be a burn of sorts. The sort of burn you get when you are well-sauced and forget you laid a cigarette down on the sink during a need-to-pee moment. Also, the kind that does not come out, no matter how hard you frantically scrub. "No problem," I say as my stomach starts to roll. "Hand me that toothpaste," I calmly request. Long story short … nothing worked. I only hoped that if we walked away, it would no longer be our problem. Lauren and I returned to the table and I readied myself for whatever news was to be announced. Bottom line: due to the weather and poor ticket sales, after taking out the rental, the food, the champagne, the staff for startup and tear down, the rental lights, etc., etc., etc. Thirty-five grand in the hole was our bottom line. No contribution to AIDS. All out of pocket.

Lauren's response was as breathtaking as it was humbling. "Well, then I forfeit my last fee. You do not have to pay me." My eyes welled-up with tears. "In fact," she reached into her purse and pulled out her Louis Vuitton checkbook and wrote a check for the deposit we paid her. "Take this and give it to the foundation. Now, I got a plane to catch before I have to head home on a fucking dogsled." We all hugged, laughed, and watched her walk down the brass-railed steps to the awaiting limousine. She turned and waved good-bye, then climbed in to the black, salt-stained car. Total class. The realization here? The quality of self-awareness removes clouded intention, allowing the soul to feel another, to see kindness in others reflected in your eyes. Do what you can when you can, if you can, and if you want, this is a pearl to be held dear and should be frequently polished with delight. Later, I would learn that the damage to the sink, not covered in the signed rental agreement, was up to us to replace. Replacing an Italian marble inlaid sink in Canadian dollars cost me around twenty thousand on top of my existing debt.

I moved out of my big apartment, moved into a wonderful studio, consolidated my debt, and made monthly payments for a year, before I realized there was no way out of all I owed without eating cat food at every meal. I bit the bullet and filed for personal bankruptcy, which removed most of my debt, and ruined my credit. Canadian student loans are not counted within bankruptcy settlements, so I owed the remainder of my education bill regardless.

I remember the day I got home after work and all my personal possessions were lost to auction. I had a bed, a TV, my sofa or chesterfield, and my clothing. My heels clicked on the newly refinished hardwood floors as I listened to Holly Cole Trio and the Indigo Girls. My tiny studio apartment was a literal manifestation of binge equals purge. I approached my business partner to borrow money against the business I had to successfully build, but was quickly informed that without me, without my hands, I had no business of value and was turned down flat. Alone, frustrated, and not knowing where to turn, I spent my last night in the salon, copying all my client's information. In the morning, I walked into my biggest competitor. The Works was located right across the street and was a burgeoning new business with established ownership. They were trendy, in the press, and in the know.

I phoned the owner, Greg, and roughly explained my plight. He was familiar with my business and the show, and all that followed. Greg assured me that I would be a welcome addition to the team and welcomed me with open arms. At that meeting, I pulled from my pocket a list of my clients and my next day's appointments. His associate manager and front-of-house receptionist contacted all, and I was to start the next morning. Change is always confusing, especially when you include others. The day was frantic. Introducing clients to such a change was as unfamiliar as it was exhilarating. After a fifteen-hour day, I had seen over forty clients and pulled in my first thousand-dollar day. My partner at the old salon was unaware and left scratching his head as to where I was. It took him a week to track down where I was and where to serve me with papers. A whole week! I signed the necessary papers and was thrilled to not be in charge. I simply took my money and went home to my little studio apartment that I rented for $295 a month. While I had downsized, I was living large and calling my own shots, without judgment or criticism from anyone other than myself. The roommate I left behind got rid of our old place and moved into my new building. Doug was a great guy. The straightest gay guy I have ever met, and I was more than happy that he was only a floor below me. We were both stylists and both a little twisted in the head. We laughed, we drank, we smoked, and yet, still went our separate ways. Christmastime was upon us and for the first time, I was attending the Famous staff Christmas party. I had heard of them through the grapevine, over-the-top food and drink and fun. This year it was held at Bob's Billiards. Oh, yes, a billiard hall. Wings, mozzarella sticks, potato skins, nachos, and all the craft beer you can drink.

In every business there is always one employee, sometimes more than one, when the universe conspires against humankind, who is a total mess. In this case, it was a girl named Lisa. Lisa looked like

Barbra Streisand, only shorter, naturally curly hair, thin and fuzzy, but the curl made it look thick. She had a prominent schnozzle to say the least, which made her look cross-eyed. She was a workout freak, so her body was trim, and she was a good stylist. She was ever-so-moody, and you did not want to be on her bad side, *ever*. Of course, she was my date for the evening. She had recently bought a new car, black, and I have no idea the make, or model, but it was a really nice car. She had purchased it only three weeks prior to the party and would be lying if I did not say I let that factor into my choices of company for the evening of Yuletide billiards and shenanigans.

The party was actually quite fun. I enjoy playing pool, but I act like I do not know what I am doing. I find it much easier to under-promise and over-deliver, and it tends to lower another's expectations. Then of course, I run the table. Beer was flowing, and at the time, the popular shot to try was a Flaming Black Sambuca. It was a process and a magic trick all in one, not a simple shot. You would tilt your head back, someone would pour the licorice-flavored spirit in your mouth, then light it on fire. You would then close your mouth; the flame would extinguish, and you would swallow the warm syrup and relish the yummy goodness. Repeat until desired effect is achieved.

Lisa really liked these, and she must have had at least a dozen. Her height and weight ratio, combined with her mental instability, contributed to her level of drunkenness. We exchanged our gifts. I do not remember what I received, but Lisa got a pair of sexy underwear from Brad. A crotch-less, black, lace thong. Lisa cooed and rushed to the bathroom. No one thought anything about her exit, but she took a little longer than expected in there. We sent Cammie in to check on her. Cammie came back and reported that Lisa was a muddled mass crying on the bathroom floor. We quickly rallied for a decision on how to handle the situation. When, suddenly, and rather unexpectedly, Lisa emerged from the bathroom, happy and acting like nothing happened. She had, however, decided to put on the panties and proceeded to give us an impromptu Victoria's Secret style fashion show. She strutted around the bar, proudly displaying her ya-ya and derriere for all to enjoy. We watched with slack jaws as Lisa made a full loop of the establishment and returned to our side of the bar. Holly embraced her, and Todd tied a shirt around her waist, lending much-needed modesty. It was time to take Lisa home. Holly took her back to the bathroom to properly attire her, and we made our exit. Lisa was hammered. I was less hammered and felt I had my wits about me enough to get her home. I left my car at the billiard hall and placed Lisa in the passenger side of her new car. All was well. She lived roughly four minutes away from where we were. So, I thought this will be a breeze. Drive Lisa to her home, catch a cab to my place, and I would pick my car up in the morning.

Driving down the icy downtown street, and like any drunk, trying to keep it together and focus on the task at hand. Following the flow of traffic, shoulder checking and driving according to the conditions.

No need guess what happened next. While following the flow of traffic, the car ahead of me decided to run a red light. I was locked on its rear end like a guidance system and never saw the light. *Wham!* A brown car carrying a Native American elder and her grandson smashed into the front end of Lisa's new car. Airbags deployed. That shit hurts.

I shook off the initial physical shock and got out of the car to assess the damage. The front end was totally pancaked, and the other car's passenger side had been clearly t-boned. I heard moaning from the other vehicle involved, and I glanced over to Lisa and checked if all was well. She informed me that she is fine, and I approach the second vehicle. I had been an Air Cadet for years, and I still have a working knowledge on the basic CPR procedure and can temporarily make a splint if needed. I looked in the window and the elderly woman is clinging to her arm, clearly in pain. The child was fine, only a little shaken. The police arrived, all sirens, all lights, all action. It was my luck that the attending officer was a good client of mine. Christine was her name. She joined me at the car; asked me if I had been drinking. She clearly smelled the sambuca on my breath. The officers did their job. Lisa was taken to the hospital for assessment, but chose to bolt out without giving a statement. In Canada, regardless of the car insurance you have, if you are under the influence during an accident, all insurance is voided. So, here I am at three in the morning, blowing a breathalyzer machine and clearly registering over any legal limits. I am charged with the DUI and phone my lawyer, who is also a client. Friend Rhonda came to pick me up, and she took me to her place where I laid on the floor to be covered in healing crystals. Rhonda is doing her waving of the hands healing, if it worked I do not know, but my father's face kept popping up in my mind. It had been over six years since I had talked with my father. Understand, in my family you were either Team Mother or Team Father. Father hardly ever said anything negative about Mother and nervously laughed at her during her times of frustration and temper tantrums. Mother, on the other hand, took great pride in telling us kids that Father was a liar, a cheat, and whatever else she could make up. So, I chose Team Mother, it was easier.

In the morning, Rhonda drives me to get my car and I make my way home. I will only have my license until my court date and my freedom will be gone that day. I sit in my apartment facing the five windows proudly displaying a view of the lake and the parliament buildings. It really was a beautiful city. Then Father's face kept eddying through my mind. I did not even know if I have his number. I decided to go against Mother's wishes and eventually track him down, thanks to Auntie Anna. She had all the info. We chatted and I explained what had happened, embarrassed and lightly broken in spirit. I tell her of my intention, and she flies into delight and encourages me to catch up with Father.

A little back story on Sharon, Dad's now-girlfriend whom he left Mother for. Those who know me will attest to the fact that I am a snooper. I will go through your bathroom cabinets and you'll be none the wiser, as I'm that good at my craft. One afternoon, while snooping in the delicate glass cupboard that *no one* was to go into except Mother, and, while I was snooping through said cupboard, I came upon a pile of letters stashed away in the back and clearly intended to be out of sight. Thankfully, my eagle-eye vision spotted them. They were letters that Sharon sent to my mother. Horrible letters demanding that Mother leave Father since she was "too fat for anybody to love." Yeah, she was that person. So, I wasn't really all cool with the fact that I had to call her to get to Dad. Putting my differences aside, I call and chat with Sharon. It is awkward at first, but she seemed genuine, warm, forthcoming, and actually pretty friendly. She handed Dad the phone and I heard his voice for the first time in six years. Pleasantries at first, and then he breaks down in tears as he tells me how much he had missed his son. He wanted to know what I was doing, how I was, and I bought it. He was a really nice guy. We decided to meet in the Hotel Regina's the next day. I felt some sense of relief and was looking forward filling in some of our six-year gap in communication.

He walked in and scanned the bar. I waved from a booth near the window. As he walked over, I noticed the same swagger that I have; I noticed his hair is much like mine in style; he was a good looking fellow. If he was not my father, I would do him. I rose and we hugged, we really hugged. He held me hard, and we connected in a very special way. It was an honest father-son embrace. He whimpered ever-so-quietly. We separated and both dragged a dry finger across our eyes, cleaning up the tender moment's tears. I tell him I am gay, he laughs, and said, "Thank God. Michael, I always knew; you are my son; that is all I care about." He asked if I was seeing anyone, who he was, what did he do, was he kind, was he good to you? I answered his questions, noting that he seems genuinely interested in me.

As this is unfolded, I also have commentary running in my mind. *Look how much time I have wasted in judgment of a person because I believed information from a secondary source. I did not choose to find out for myself, actually ask the person judged regarding the information I used to judge.* My conscience shook a finger at me, and I vowed never to do it again.

We had a few drinks and a most pleasant time. He invited me to his house to meet Sharon, and since Ukrainian Christmas was around the corner, I would catch up with Dad's side of the family, my cousins, my uncles. These were people we were not allowed to see since their divorce. Mother would have a fit if she knew that I had agreed to put in an appearance and "rejoin" the family I had ignored for years. The party was surprisingly wonderful. Homemade Ukrainian food was plentiful, and I had missed that so much. Vodka, home brew, Labatt's Blue, Crown Royal, my dad's side of the family really knew how to have a good time. It was incredibly nice to catch up with cousins I had forgotten I had. I drank with the family and smoked a joint with my favorite uncle in the garage. I sat on the ski-doo as he rested against the 1967 Chevy he was restoring. In the far-left corner was a deer hanging upside down with the head removed. It was skinned, the feet removed, and it was quietly draining of its red humor before it was made into steaks, ribs, roasts, and the like. We passed the joint back and forth while. We drank Dad's special brew that tasted like water. It would creep up slowly and smack you in the back of the head and elevated you to a state where inhibitions dissolved. Uncle was smiling and laughing and looking very enticing. My preference is men who are a little older. I fear with the mix of smoke, brew, and my preoccupation, a situation may come up. He was explaining where he was when the now-hanging deer was shot, and I noticed the fly of his pants is open. I noticed the outline of his fun stick and easily developed a mental image. We walked toward the animal, and I noticed the shape of his ass through is very worn Wranglers. I wanted to feel him. I wanted him. However, he was my dad's brother. I cleared my head and politely dismiss myself using the need of the bathroom excuse. He says to me, "Just pee here, there is a drain over here." He proceeded to undo his buttoned Wranglers and freed himself. Do I look? Is he doing this on purpose? I wanted to look! I look. Very nice. Very, very nice, indeed.

Imagery in tow, I had to bail. "I'm good, I'm heading back inside, catch ya later. Nice chat!" In hindsight, I should have never left that garage. Who knows what bad things I would have done. In hindsight, getting the DUI was the best thing that happened to me.

With all the change, Doug, the former roommate, now downstairs neighbor, and I decided to take a vacation together. Our choice was Vancouver, British Columbia. A delectable sea side city with and active gay lifestyle that resembled Amsterdam, minus the red-light district. We walked the Sea Wall, shopped on Robson Street, and partied on Davie. Shower Power at Bubbles featured live nude male dancers in four showers hovering over the dancing crowd. Water would come on, he would soap up, and most times, masturbate for the crowd during a random round of shots, rinse off, then go back to bartending. Think dinner theatre, but with nudity. Back then, the drug that the party kids were taking was called SpecialK. It was a horse tranquilizer that when ingested made you very free; you had all the energy in the world, and it heightened your sensory appreciation. You enjoyed the sensation of touching and being touched. I never took it. It kind of scared me, but I did enjoy watching a sea of shirtless men, sweating and grinding. Sitting, sipping my double Grey Goose and grapefruit I scanned the crowd. I was on holiday and a little fling would not hurt. Doug was a fan of SpecialK, so he was doing what you do in the middle of the dance floor. Doug was sexy, but he was the brother I never had. I found it impossible to see him in a sensual manner.

Then, standing in the shadows in the corner is this tall guy wearing white, tight-fitting jeans, a light-blue linen shirt unbuttoned to the belly button, and cowboy boots. He looked like a cross between Dennis Quaid and Patrick Swayze. We made eye contact, and he walked over. A bit gay-swishy, but tolerable. He had everything right: the drinks, the conversation, the knee touching, and a couple of whispering in the ear moments. This guy was rocking my world. We danced, he was very fit. Thank god I had recently gone through a depression … I had lost some weight so I did not look bad in a Speedo. I felt him, aroused, and pressed against my left leg. He seemed sizeable and workable. Kissing happened; he was good. Then he asked if we could continue in the privacy of my room. Now, I am sharing the room with Doug, who I know will be dancing through the wee hours of the night and morning. There was a possibility that we could go back, have some fun together, and he could leave before Doug made it back to the room. It was only a short walk from the club to the hotel, so that was certainly plausible. Ironically, I played the good boy and reluctantly declined. Even as he persisted, I held strong, and we went our separate ways. When I get home, I continued to talk to the new sexy man. His name was Sydney. He was a banker and was studying to become an Episcopalian minister. I thought that was very interesting. Someone who thinks of things as a whole and follows the word of God. Even though I am not a fan of organized religion, I thought I could learn something new, and hell, it would not kill me to go to church. We talked endlessly on the phone. He lived in Seattle and I was living in Regina. This was long before free long distance was even a possibility, and the long-distance telephone bills were insane. Months passed and Sydney, a.k.a. New Sexy Man, decided to come to wintery Regina. During that time, we consummated our relationship and I found myself falling in love. He was HIV positive and took tons of medication. I will say this, if you really want to know how to have safe sex, date someone with HIV. I did extensive research and learned that transmission was easy enough to avoid if you were diligent. So, we applied this learning and had a very satisfying sexual relationship. His mind was very deep, and we had long talks about the state of things and how we processed the information. How to take any situation and find the pearl … find the lesson … of course, this made him more and more attractive. One day, Doug and I were talking and he revealed to me that he was getting involved rather seriously with this guy living in Vancouver, and he was honestly considering moving west. After a bottle of Jameson's and a couple joints, Doug and I realized that a change would be fun. The two of us could afford a better apartment, and we both had money stashed away that would cover us until we were gainfully employed. We had nothing keeping us in Regina, and we were sick of the frigging winters. We were moving. I told Dad I was thinking of moving West with Doug, and he thought it was a wonderful idea. He and Sharon had never been to Vancouver. So, they offered to move me out West. They had a trailer and we loaded it with my belongings; the plan was to drive me out to my new life. We actually did it. Eighteen hours cooped up with a father I was genuinely getting to know again, and the woman for which he left my mother. This could be good; this could be bad. It was fun. We stayed in a couple hotels along the way, and we had a great time as we learned about each other. I eventually warmed up to Sharon, although I did not trust her completely. I do not recall the exact reasons for my distrust, it was a lingering feeling about her, but she was tolerable.

We drove first to Seattle and met Sydney; we explored the place I would be spending my time during the weekends. I had proposed to

Sydney during his stay with me in Regina. So technically, Sydney was my fiancé. My weekend home sat on Lake Washington. You could see Bill Gates' house from our front yard. The apartment was only four hundred square feet. You had to exit the bathroom to turn around, but the view was stunning. Floor-to-ceiling windows picture-framed the lake, and the loons would serenade us in the evenings. Very *on golden pond*. So there I was, in one of the most beautiful cities in the country. My weekday home was a one-bedroom apartment, on the twentieth floor, with a futon in the living room for my bedding area since I was away on weekends, and Doug took the bedroom. We had a small galley kitchen and a sizeable bathroom. The dining room was tiny, but we had more windows than walls. Our wrap around balcony offered views of Grandville Island, the cityscape, and the most majestic view of the Pacific Ocean I had seen. On overcast, rainy days, clouds would cover everything, leaving only a perfect view of Whistler mountain. It was like you could step on the clouds; *heavenly* is the best word for it. I eventually found work at an Elizabeth Arden Red Door Spa and Salon in the Pacific Center. It was a new salon offering great benefits and the prestige of working for the woman who was a trailblazer in the beauty industry. I considered it to be a great honor. Doug worked at the chair next to me. So at least I there was a familiar face close.

Industry Fun Fact: Every time a stylist moves, even if it is a mile away from the location they worked, you lose 20 percent of your clientele. I had moved and had to start all over again, build a whole new book of clients. This would take time. I folded more towels, washed more color bowls, cleaned more shampoo traps than I care to mention. The other stylists came with full books and were industry veterans. A few warmed up to me instantly and we had a great time. A few found me as a threat since I was young, talented, not bad to look at, and I was new enough to drink the corporate Kool-Aid. I knew which ass to kiss, and this ability, not necessarily a use of my powers of manipulation, could underscore that I was merely a company team player. I did not care. I worked hard and was accepted to be on the Core One Training Team for the company. This gave me special privileges. I took special classes with top makeup artists, color specialists, and some of the best cutters I had ever seen. This old dog was learning new tricks and loving it. I was getting and retaining more and more clients, and things were falling into place. On the weekends, I would catch the train and head down to see Sydney. We would go to dinner, walk along the river, and talk, and then have some mind-blowing fun time. During the week, we would talk on the phone. However, every now and again, when I would call at one in the morning, he would not answer. I let it go a few times, and finally asked him one weekend. "How come when I call sometimes, all I get is the machine. What's up with that?" *I was sleeping* was his excuse. All right. That could be, but we generally chatted during these hours. My spider sense was tingling. My arrival time leading into our weekends was usually at 6:45 p.m. at SeaTac. On this particular evening pick up, Sydney arrived totally smashed. It was very out of the ordinary. He had a glass of wine once in a while, but with his looming minister training, he was a good boy. We did go to church on Sundays. Let me tell you, the Episcopalian services are like a religious drag show. The cast are all in costume: one is carrying a candle, the other swings something burning that fills the church with choking smoke. Stand up, sit down, repeat. Say these lines three hundred times. Stand up, sit down. Then everyone gathers around scorching hot coffee in polystyrene cups making idle chitchat. My brain would not shut up most Sundays. *What a load of hooey,* I thought. However, this one Sunday, we could not attend church. Sydney had a work event or training or something, and I had the apartment all to myself. "That's okay, I will clean." I said. The place was four hundred square feet. Cleaning went quickly.

    Before I proceed, I have to share something of which I am not proud, and no longer need conceal it. I am a snooper. If you invite me into your home, I will go through everything in your bathroom. I believe all I need to know about you is located in your medicine cabinet and under the sink. There, I said it. So, while cleaning the bookshelf, I noticed what appeared to be a journal. I opened the book and sure enough, it was Sydney's diary. Who the hell keeps a diary anymore? I put the book back and headed outside for a cigarette, seemingly leaving temptation behind. Should I read it? No, that would be an invasion of privacy. No, I will not read it. But it's right there. If he did not want you to see it, he should have hidden it better. I am going to look. *No, Michael, that is wrong.* But I want to. DO. NOT. DO. IT. MICHAEL. I pick up the journal again. I put it down. I walk to the kitchen. I walk back to the book. I pick it up. I put it down. I sit in the wooden rocker and look out the window onto the beautiful lake. I hear the buzz of saws over at Bill's house; he is renovating. So peaceful. I rock for a few minutes and contemplate what I am going to learn and the fear of that knowledge. I pick up the journal and head outside to the dock. I begin to read. I know what I am doing is wrong. Well, let me make a long story short: the reason I could not reach him at 1 in the morning was he was in the gay park providing services to passersby. Fourteen other men. One with the most perfect golden retriever who drove a red jeep. He was mentioned in many entries. Sydney wished I had more money and felt that he would have to break up the engagement, eventually. I read and read and read. Page after page of sexual escapades … I had been duped. What to do, what to do? I was broken. How the hell does a gay priest with HIV find this behavior acceptable, plausible even?

Hell, I logged many hours during numerous doctor appointments genuinely concerned for his white and red cell counts. What was his viral load this week? Were there any alterations to the medications needed? What else was transpiring in his secret world? Which other STDs were possibly in the mix with his HIV?

What to do? He would be home in an hour. What to do? Well, I chose. I opened the journal to the last page and wrote, "Thanks, and go fuck yourself." Juvenile, I know. I took off my ring and placed it on the page. Called a cab and I took an earlier train back to Vancouver. Days passed with no word from Sydney. I cried and cried. Even at work, I cried. Friday came. I finished early and walked the ten blocks home, stopped, and picked up some wine and salmon sushi. Standing on the balcony, wine stoically in hand, I heard the buzzer. It was Sydney. You know what my stomach did. Calm bowels in the past, he came in, I poured him a glass of wine, and we retreated to the beautiful city panorama. Total silence. Not a word. Then he slides the ring I bought him from his finger and hands it to me. I was not crushed; I was beneath my own feet. Underfoot and broken. I took the ring and watched it fall as I released it from our twentieth floor landing. I reached over and took his wine glass, put my hand on his shoulder, and proceeded to lead him to the door he came through. He walked through and turned to me. I closed the door. Not one word was uttered.

Doug was away. So I had the place to myself that night. I drank my wine and found a nice piece of chocolate in the freezer. It was Doug's, but I knew he would not mind. I turned all the lights off, the illumination from the busy city lights barely finding their way in the small apartment. I prayed that one day I would be worthy enough to find someone who valued me, and I realized that I needed to become that person.

As I laid on the futon, I closed my eyes and saw the most wonderful lights in my head. I opened my eyes and the light was still there. It was dancing all around me, and I could actually feel the radiant shimmer. I knew I was not intoxicated enough for this, and I did not know what I was seeing and experiencing. Was this the lord? Was this pure energy? Pictures of people, places, situations all came flooding through. The pictures would come from the left, zoom right in front of me, stop for a second so I could recall that time, then it would slide away. Then one would come from the right side and do the same thing. This went on for what must have been hours. I awoke to the door opening. It was approaching noon, if not already passed, and Doug was home. I could not wait to tell him what happened. He would be so proud of me. Then I remembered my realization experience. Doug was a deep enough thinker to not only understand, he would be fascinated. We exchanged pleasantries, and I started to make coffee as Doug liberated ice from the freezer for one of his smoothie concoctions.

"Hey? Did you see a little foil packet in here? I can't find it." He searched with his head in the freezer.

"Yeah …" I confessed. "I was craving chocolate, and I found that leftover piece of a Toblerone, and I ate it, sorry." Busted.

"You owe me forty bucks," he declared.

My confused look warranted the follow up, "That wasn't Toblerone you ass."

"What do you mean?" My indiscretion was forgotten. He had my attention.

"That was shrooms hidden in some chocolate. How high did you get? You are only supposed to have a quarter at a time. Did you eat the whole thing?" So much for divine intervention and insight from the mother spirit. Forty bucks for Doug and his magic chocolate.

Here I am—new city, new job, no lover, great apartment; one block from the grocery store, fresh market, dry cleaners, liquor store, and a cozy jazz bar just off the back alley; two blocks to the ocean and seawall, and a two-minute water taxi ride to Grandville Island. Grandville was similar to a farmers' market with some of the finest artisan items: jewelry, clothing, and some of the best food I have ever had.

Introspection: repeat a process that had thus far worked for me. Dedicating myself to building my business; the business of me.

There were many ways to jump start this new venture. During my downtime, and if all towels and color bowls were cleaned, I would go down to the makeup counters. Make friends with a few that weren't too weird and do mini hair makeovers between makeup applications. I also had a certain finesse of doing five-minute style changes to the passersby. The quicker you can change someone's look, the easier they think it is for them to do themselves. I chose the possible victims that looked to be in the upper median income range, knowing that they had disposable income.

The grand opening was coming up. Elizabeth Arden had spent over three million dollars on the new renovation and in order to launch it, we had to put on a little dog-and-pony show. I was consumed with last-minute details to ensure a great opening. We were stationed at the entrance to greet the incoming crowd. The stage housed three industry professionals, one color technician, one precision cutter, and one makeup artist all doing mini make-overs on people watching us from the floor. After their forty-five minutes on stage, there was a forty-five-minute fashion show featuring the fine fashions modeled by the better-looking staff from Pacific Center. Luckily, Vancouver is filled with models, actors, and performers; and they worked in Pacific Center. During the show, I, or our guest professional, would hop on stage and demonstrate a transition style, or mystify the crowd with the multiple styles and versatility of the cut. In retail displays, whether its lipstick, shoes, or even a demonstration, you have four seconds to grab someone's interest. If they stay longer, they are interested, if you hold their attention for three minutes, you rarely lose the individual as a customer. The professional they were sending was touted as one of the best. His name was Steven McGraw from the King of Prussia in Pennsylvania, one of the largest malls in America. He resembled Michael Douglas but with blond hair. He was a member of the Core One training team, was a five-year company veteran, and was traveling to other Elizabeth Arden locations giving a seminar called How to Make a Thousand Dollars a Day. The show was two days away and he was to arrive in a few hours. I placed his photo in the stand-up placard in the entrance of the salon and random places throughout the store. Then, I went back to the salon and waited for Mr. Wonderful. Well … the swagger Steven McGraw had was one of unbridled confidence. He was tanned and highlighted, tailored in an Armani suit, a French cuffed shirt, and a Zenya tie. He walked in like he owned the joint. Oh, I liked it; I liked it, I did. Sunny was my manager, she and Steve made and instant connection. I was introduced, and greeted Mr. I'm too Good for You, Look at My Eyes, See My Smile, with a firm handshake. I really wanted him to prove to me that my judgment of instant disdain was accurate, but instead, I made eye contact with the bluest eyes I had ever seen. His smile was warm, contradicting his brazen demeanor. We held each other's gaze, then broke at the same time. Both in realization that there were others watching us. We convened our meeting and discussed the details of the show. Everything from where we would enter to what was on the music list was covered. Steve's several suggestions that were very clever and all business. Models were filtering through to go over their hair and makeup looks. Final fittings, be that as it may. Minutiae were dispensed with accordingly. All in all, we were ready. With the day's business at an end, Sunny, Steve, and I decided to go to The Victorian. The Victorian was a spectacular historic hotel that was impeccably refurbished. Every detail was restored to its original splendor. It was a fabulous venue to delve into that-which-was Steve. Over several Bombay Sapphire dirty martinis; we learn Steve is originally from as small town close to the Du Pont factories. He is one of eight children, very Brady Bunch-like. He had been published. He had prepared platform work for some of the greats, and he was the national marketing director for North America for Arden. I was impressed … the man had street credit. As we eased into the evening hours, we finished our social Q & A session. I needed to put some last-minute effort into my opening to insure it was flawless, and I was now inclined to show-off for Mr. Wonderful. Sunny wobbled her way to the washroom; the woman could not hold her liquor. As we mutter best wishes for surviving her restroom excursion, Steve slid next to me, and he said, "You know, I could really use some help finishing up my presentation for tomorrow. Would you be interested?" I should not have been so shocked with his forwardness, but I was. "I would love to, but I have got so many working pieces in my opening, I really have to work on that." Who was I kidding, of course, I wanted to go upstairs to his room; of course, I wanted to do nasty things. I mean, hell, I was thin and still had a good ass. I didn't know if I wanted to kiss him or slap him, but I knew I did want to touch things I shouldn't. Why do you always judge your actions, Michael? "Even for an hour?" he persisted. Any other time, any other place, I would have leapt at this chance. He was handsome, sexy; and for sounding like such a queer, there was a very masculine side that gave me instant false comfort. His ego, which normally is a total boner killer for me, was ironically attractive. My problem? He was management. I was new with the company, and I did not want to screw that up. My thoughts digressed: *What the hell? What could possibly go wrong? Could I sleep my way to the top? Ugh, then I would be one of those people. Do I care what people think of me? Do I care about how I think of myself?* "I really have to get back, I'm a bit anal retentive and a type A personality, so, gotta take a pass on this one," was my mission statement. As I walked home, I was both happy with myself and proud of my maturity. Nonetheless, now I was horny. Damn. The show was seamless. The opening went well, my opening model, who was fourteen, stood tall at six feet, and was gorgeous. We had diligent audience participation, and Steve was really smart here. He would scan the crowd for a group of women who were clearly together for an outing. Profiling has its place. These were women who lunched, had a little nosh, got mani-pedis before getting a Brazilian wax; they shopped, then had a little drinky-poo before they headed back to their mansions in the hills. He would pluck one out for a quick change so her friends would stay longer and give testament to the before and after. Worked every time.

We had a great crowd. Many stayed for the whole show. Afterward, Steve was offering free consultations at the salon with the intention to lace the appointment book with solutions to said consultations. I graced the overflow with a tour of the spa area, of the mud room, of the steam room, and of the facial and massage rooms. Ever seeking to impress and garner a booking, we worked very well together.

We booked over $30,000 in services, and we sold close to $11,000 in retail product as a result of the four-hour exhibition. It was the best learning experience I had been a part of as a professional. I learned a new dance that day. Finessing and directing, without pushing.

Our triumph was complete, and the day was over. We congratulated each other for jobs well done.

Sunny looked like she was pulled through a keyhole backward. Her eyeliner was smudged, her lashes were caked with mascara, only the outline of her lips remained. She went home. "Can I buy you dinner?" Steve asked. "I would really like that. I know a great new place, and a friend of mine works there."

My friend Roger was a WAM (waiter, actor, model) with a smoking body, a great smile, a kind heart, and zero intelligence. During an evening filled with sangria and a few toots, we asked Roger if he ordered a large pizza, would he rather have it cut up in eight pieces, or twelve pieces. He said he'd have it cut in eight pieces because there was no way he could eat twelve pieces by himself. Enter hysterical laughter. I mean laughter where you can't catch your breath and leaves your sides sore. I loved the guy and finally had to get my big paint brushes out and paint a picture of the problem. I really don't think he ever understood it. A good guy though. I think he was from Brazil.

We walked five blocks to Davie Street to friend Roger's work place Sans Souci, whose name translated is "Without Anxiety," or "Carefree." As we walked, we chatted about his family, my family, how I got involved with Arden, my career experience, etc.

The walk was enjoyable. Once at the restaurant, Roger showed us to our table. I ordered a double of Jameson's, on the rocks. Steve ordered a double of Grey Goose with grapefruit juice. I thought, that bitch ordered my signature cocktail.

Vancouver is a fishing industry town. The seafood is always fresh and delicious. Roger returned with our drinks, informed us of the specials, and recommended the seafood sampler appetizer, it was perfect for two people he concluded.

Steve maintained the professional wall needed to push through in our industry. Like any corporately run business, there are unwritten rules, and only those on the rise with serious potential to claim the top roles know and apply them correctly. Our corporate macrocosm does not want you to think on the clock; our corporate time clock was reserved for creating satisfied repeat customers and something about hair. Unsurprisingly, if you took enough of your own time and initiative to properly lay out a system of improvement, and you can prove its possible efficiency to produce continual results, that is a different story. We knew the system, the rules, and the game. We knew how to meander, how to pander, and how to ponder, all the while looking flawless and cutting some incredible hair. Neither one of us kissed ass overzealously, and neither one of us took any shit. The idea of attaching my wagon to this horse was looking better and better. We were both hard workers who were good at our craft, and we both came from small towns where being gay was not appreciated like it is today.

As we found our comfort zones with each other, Steve let more of his guard down. He was truly delightful.

Roger appeared with our appetizers.

I mentioned how fresh the seafood was in Vancouver, right? Well, half of the appetizer plate was still moving, and the other half was moaning. Roger sat the plate between us. Steve and I looked at each other, then looked at what should have been studied rather than eaten. "Roger, honey, my love … this isn't going to work. We'll just take the check," I declared.

We walked back to his hotel, sat in its lounge at the bar, and we ordered two cheeseburgers. After several more libations, I switched to my grapefruit Goose spirit animal, and we talked for hours, several to be exact. Knees were touching, he was leaning in, he would rub the dimple that resided in the same place as Michael Douglas. His warm breath had the essence of alcohol, something I find oddly really sexy and before I knew it his hand was working its way up my thigh firmly, yet childishly seeking approval. He was really charming, and I am a sucker for a man in a suit. Grab your pearls and act surprised, I slept with him that night.

His suit had lied to me, blatantly. The man had no ass, but his class reigned true. Waiting for us in his room was a bottle of champagne on ice with, yes, fresh strawberries. He had called from the restaurant and arranged it. Premeditated confidence at its finest, and that was it. I conceded to the swoon. It was an incredibly fun night.

The next day was filled with three mini seminars in other Arden locations in the area. A little hung over, always professional, we drudged through the day. At its end, Sunny and I drove Steve to the airport. I had to admit, I was a bit sad to see him go. His flight was called, and we three headed to the gate. He gave Sunny a big hug and a kiss on the cheek. As she turned to check her phone, Steve and I embraced firmly. "I'm going to call you very soon." "I was hoping you'd say that." We kissed, no tongue. A tender taste of future possibilities; it tasted like pineapple. He turned back to wave one final time; it was as picturesque as a Burberry centerfold in *GQ*.

Sunny dropped me off at home. Exhausted and exhilarated translated into clear confusion. My phone rings, "Guess where I'm calling from?" Steve was such a nerd, but there is something kind of cool from calling from thirty thousand feet flying at four hundred miles an hour. I always feel so continental.

Our grand opening was held in May. By the middle of June, we had come to know each other in some depth. We missed each other terribly, and Steve suggested that I come to Delaware for a weekend stay. He paid for my ticket. How could I say no?

When I arrived in Philly, Steve was at the airport to greet me. My excitement was throbbing if you know what I mean. I tried to cool my jets; maybe once on his turf, I'd see the real Steve. Maybe he was a total douche bag who ate with his feet while watching football and farting at every touchdown. Then rounds the corner and I meet his gaze. The eyes are the same, the swagger is the same, the smile is the same, and he was looking mighty fine in his Levi's. I hoped I wasn't wrong on this one. Inappropriate gropes were instinctual as we walked to his red Toyota Forerunner, Limited Edition (whatever that means).

He did not mention it, but as we walked, I silently took note of Saran wrap on his arm covering what appeared to be a barbed-wire tattoo. We dispatched my luggage. Once we were settled into the SUV, we kissed passionately.

When our physical needs were met for the moment, the kissing tenderly faded.

Steve broke the silence with, "Look at my new tattoo! Kiss it!" I was focused on the tattoo at that point, although a little put off by the request.

I questioned, "You're serious?"

"Yeah, kiss it," he encouraged.

"There's no fucking way I'm kissing a fresh tattoo covered in Vaseline," I countered.

"Good, I wouldn't either," he laughed. He was an ass or that was a great save. His home was quaint and keenly decorated with a motherly feeling. Ornaments abounded. Plant life was everywhere; ferns, elephant ear plants, fresh-cut flowers. Hutches were filled with china and crystal stemware. The walls were well papered and always complimented the robin's egg-blue carpet. He led me through the house and on to the back deck. It was a spectacular outdoor oasis with traveling trumpet vines, wisteria, clematis, and magnolias that accented the lattice surround. The deck overlooked an oval in-ground pool, graciously accepting water from a ten-foot fountain that floated in the middle. Steve had a large table set very elegantly outside on the deck, a bottle of Jordan Chardonnay was open and ready to serve. We dined on filet and lobster. Dessert was tiramisu. Okay, he cooks, too, and has an inkling how to use his gay spray decorating talents. We dined and laughed and drank. He suggested we take a dip in the deep end, double entendre noted and received. I reminded him that for safety's sake, we should wait the mandatory thirty minutes before swimming. Whatever would we do to make the time pass?

My personal trainer at the time was this bitch named Depression, and I was slim. Slim enough at least to think I could pull off a Speedo and enjoy the sex appeal that swimming attire tends to generate. It worked. We swam, played around, and then retired for the night. We left our dirty dishes in the sink. Not something I would normally do, but hell, it was his house. It was about 90 degrees out on a beautiful summer night. We dried off and made our way into the frozen tundra. Steve's internal temperature always ran hot, and he kept the air conditioning at around 62 degrees. Froze my butt off as I slipped on the laminate floor, slightly twisting my knee in the process. Oh, yeah, I'm smooth. In the bedroom, I will say there was little sleep. The next morning, I woke to an intoxicating sound. I opened my eyes and connected sound with scene. Outside the patio doors, I could see the fountain making the water in the pool dance. I rolled over and explored Steve as I moved closer. He was warm to the touch and had sprouted some major morning wood. You can ponder what happened next.

As we laid in bed, I caught my breath. Still lightheaded from my post-coital bliss, I heard a noise in the kitchen. Someone was washing dishes. I also noticed the smell of coffee. "Is someone in the kitchen?" I ask.

Steve swiftly moved to check his watch. "Oh, that's just Janet," he replied. "Come, I want you to meet her." He quickly dressed, I donned my Speedo, and we made our way to the kitchen. In the kitchen stood a short, redheaded woman with brown-rimmed glasses drying the last gold-rimmed Mikasa dinner plate.

"I thought I'd just give you a hand," said the short, red-haired, brown-glass wearing, female intruder. I was taken a bit by surprise and humbled to be seen by a total stranger in my new bathing attire.

Steve greeted her with a hug, and I opted for an introductory handshake. After all, I am semi-clad and sporting the end stage of a very healthy erection.

"This is Janet Hughes. She was the first client I ever had in hair school, and she still comes to me. Sunday is wash and blow-dry day." After I expressed my joy in meeting her, I headed out for a dip in the pool. My pride and morals in tow, I knew she heard what we had done.

Ugh. Oh well.

The weekend came to an end and we continued to learn more and more about each other. We spent the day at Rehoboth beach which is a cleaner Atlantic City. We played games, rode rides, ate well, had several libations, and seemed to always be laughing. His dry sense of humor was right up my alley *plus*, always a good tell about the integrity of a person, Steve was very kind to waiters. He knew what would happen if he wasn't—instant spit in the food. Steve drove me to the airport and dropped me at the gate. He kissed passionately then I walked backward and waved as he pulled away in the red Fore Runner. A good time was had by all.

I could truly see myself with this man long-term. Location would be an issue.

Eventually, after three weeks apart, Steve and I discussed living together. Steve lobbied for a transfer to Vancouver as he fell in love with the city during his time there. Our company policy was transferring could occur within the employee's originating division only. For example, if you worked for the Saks Fifth Avenue division, you could only transfer to another Saks. If you worked for the Bloomingdale division, you could only transfer to another Bloomingdale's. Steve was Bloomingdale's, I was Saks. In the face of Steve's persistence, and in response to corporate's reluctance to move Steve from his market, the company countered with an offer of me making the transfer since my clientele was not that of my cohort's. In all honesty, Steve was one of the top money makers for the company. Our corporate overlords would lose less money.

I sold everything I could not fit in my luggage. I literally packed up my troubles in the old kit bag. I am not sure if I smiled at the turn of fate. I am not even sure if I remembered to put on a fake one at best. I was scared shitless.

I made the move to Delaware. I even flew my two cats to Steve's house in advance. Those damn cats flew first class apparently; it was stupidly expensive.

I made it to Steve's, a.k.a., our home, after twelve hours and nineteen stops. I am guessing my tickets were closer to ten dollars. Fucking cats. He opened the door with an incredibly dashing smile that framed his wonderful eyes. I bounded up the stairs into his arms. After our embrace and the ushering in of my luggage, his hyper activity disorder went into overdrive. He pulled me into one of the three bedrooms and introduced me to my new armoire. A closet full of Calvin Klein, Donna Karan, Boss, Ralph Lauren, what was at least thirty ties, socks for days, shoes to match, and complete with undershirts. I was floored. *All this? For me?* No one ever had been this kind or supportive. Of course, I had to lie on my back for a spell. I felt the need to give back, if you know what I mean. It was glorious. If this was any indication of how my life is going to be, I would gladly take it, and I would do it with a smile on my face.

I arrived on a Saturday. Sunday, Steve and I were invited to a dry run of the new Elizabeth Arden Red Door Spa and Salon in New York, then on to the World Hair Awards right down the street. Seeing the new renovations of the new and improved Red Door was fun, but still all smoke and mirrors. Fancy food, and a lot of bullshit, ego-driven, look-at-me feelings. The WHA was spectacular. Top industry professionals from the big hair product companies were there and doing some really excellent hair. The production quality of these shows was incredibly impressive.

The hair cosmos within a major city, especially on the high end of the spectrum, is riddled with complication, addiction, self-mutilation, and confusion, all wrapped up in a pretty professional package. The industry is completely ego-driven. It is an art form, and truth be told, most artists are narcissistic assholes. Not the whole lot, there are the few ideologues that still believe in making the client happy. You truly have to find your happy medium. In the echelons of wealthy salon regulars, word travels incomprehensibly fast. You must be excellent at your job at this point. The higher the price of the haircut, the higher the expectation placed on you. Your last haircut may end up being your last haircut. Once "Iris" tells "Gloria" what you did to her hair, at best your clients are now gun shy, or at worst you are fucked. In order to survive the profession's customer complaint grapevine, or "Iris's" fat mouth, is an amalgamation of flattery and ass-kissery needed for major spin-doctoring. You have to be able to control and reverse as much damage as humanly possible in such a situation.

I want take this time to give you an industry insight to the high-end salon experience: the stylist's charges will more than likely be reflective of the level shit the client tends to give said stylist. A stylist-imposed stress tax if you please.

We operated a level below the weathering wealthier salon regulars. At $65 dollars a cut, we were affordable enough to appeal to a wider market. We did well with our add-on services, usually up-selling to a spa or nail service. If Gloria started out coming to me only for haircuts, I would make sure I introduced her to my professional cohorts. Gloria would, in time, or rather swiftly, discover she can pamper herself once a month for under $200.

If Gloria booked a day in the salon with us, Gloria would go first for her facial. Next, Gloria would come to me for a deep conditioning that would be left in while her manicure was attended. Then, back to me for a cut and blow dry. We were fun, always with an intelligent quip, and we always dressed in a suit and tie. We were an experience that returned Gloria to the world with a better outlook. She looked and felt great about herself. That was our goal.

Sunday was our only off day. Thankfully, there was a Texas Roadhouse near our development. On any given Sunday there were all the blooming onions you could eat. We would go over around one, sit at the bar, drink beer, harass the male bartenders, and have a bite before we would head back home before we were long in the evening hours. If you missed it, on any given Sunday, we got trashed.

We cycled through each week's stresses and successes five strong years, and narcissistic assholery aside, we were good.

Steve and I lived together, we worked together, we drove the hour and a half each way to and from said work together, we shopped together, we vacationed together. There was a lot of together time.

We never seemed to really get on each other's nerves that much. There was a mutual respect that we treasured; however, we both weren't a person to sit on our hands and keep our mouth shut. Steve was infamous for flying off the handle. Whether with me, a coworker or even a client, if you pissed him off, you got the wrath of Steve. At the King of Prussia location, I was his manager. Now, imagine reprimanding your lover over a situation with a client. I did it though, and I got better at pointing out and having him realize he'd been a total asshole and needed to address the issue. He didn't like it, I didn't like doing it, but he would totally walk all over you if you let him. I do feel that he did respect me more for doing so.

I was with Steve for fourteen years. The first five were really wonderful. We made money, we spent money, we bought things, ate out at great restaurants, we traveled to Jamaica twice, we enjoyed our lives. As a couple, we never fell on hard times. There were a few years of cocaine, partying a little too hard, jealousy, and dents in the floor caused by a very frustrating time. Steve had a true talent for hearing you, then switching your words around to make his argument. This infuriated me, and in turn, I applied the "I'm sorry you feel that way." This picked his ass. At the end of the day, I loved him and he loved me.

Steve and I always found fun; sometimes dangerous fun. We had season tickets to the opera, we attended openings of private art showings, and on more than one occasion, were able to work our way behind the stage and meet such people as Nora Jones, the band YES, and Barry Manilow. Hat's off to Scotch. Hell, we had a collection of straight-guy underwear, trophies from those questioning and giving into curiosity's temptation to experience a sexual unknown for one night.

One Sunday in July, I believe, we kept with our routine and made our way to the Roadhouse. This day, we found ourselves sitting next to what had to be at least eight bikers. New Jersey bikers. The real kind. The more they drank, the rowdier they became. I feared for our lives since we weren't looking like anything but two gay guys who showered and did our hair before our afternoon excursion. The more Steve drank, the more talkative he became and his fear level becomes nonexistent in a short period of time. This began to really trouble me and I felt increasingly uncomfortable. I'm not really the fighting type. We all did shots of Tequila, and, as fate would have it, one of the more jovial, and fuzzier, bikers took a liking to Steve. So much so, Steve was propositioned to take a ride with him on his bike. We laughed, joked around, and sloughed it off. Furry was persistent if not forward. He could see the hesitancy in wanting to further homogenize with their group and proceeded to grab Steve's hand and put it on his crotch. "You can hold this while I drive," he offered.

"Let me think about it for a bit," Steve said.

*Seriously?* Even in my drunken state of being, I could see no-good written all over the possible chain of events if Steve acquiesced. By all means, go with at total stranger who is two hundred pounds larger than you, covered in hair from his eyeballs to his asshole, who has been drinking boilermakers all afternoon, and on a Harley, knowing full well Steve generally freaks out when a bug falls into his lap. I subtly pinched Steve on the arm to get his attention. "There's no fucking way you're even considering this, right?" I do not think I unclenched my teeth to let the inaudible growl of a question out.

"Come on, I think it would be fun." Dangerous fun indeed.

"Okay, you do that. I'm heading home. Good luck with fuzzy wuzzy." Against my better judgment, I got up and walked the two blocks home, fuming every step of the way. Each step was fueled by the anger I had about his stupidity, him getting a little overly friendly with someone who really looked like Chewbacca, and the obvious fear that I may never see him again. He struggled through the door an hour and a half later. He collapsed on the stairs and sobbed tears of pain and confusion. He looked broken and weak, both physically and mentally. Not a good look and a look that I've never seen him wear. I turned into recovery mode and start to calmly ask him what had transpired. "What happened? Are you okay?" My mind was an eddy of worst-case scenarios.

Steve had politely declined Fuzzy-Wuzzy's proposition and left the bar no more than five minutes after I had. It had taken over an hour for him to traverse the two blocks home. On his way home, Steve's right leg gave out. It was not the average inebriation induced footing and balance failure. Steve could not lift his leg normally. He had literally crawled the two blocks home.

Our initial grasp of the situation led us to surmise that it was a product of the liquor, hot weather, and an essentially empty stomach. We made an appointment with his old doctor and was able to see him on Monday. We sat in the fluorescent light and the shag-carpeted office that was graciously fragranced by the overpowering smell of lilacs found only a bottle of extremely cheap perfume. Lilac herself informed us that the doctor would see Steve now. I'm not sure what the doctor could offer, or what information we expected to hear, but this doctor clearly had no idea whether to scratch his watch or wind his butt. We left, and we agreed to find someone with a little more knowledge. After a figurative shit storm of doctors, blood tests, MRIs, CAT scans, specialists, strength tests, spinal taps, we finally meet Dr. Greenstein, head of neurology at Christiana hospital in Philadelphia, Pennsylvania. He was a tall man, with a freshly-boiled and shiny complexion. The man had no bedside manner. He was blunt. He was direct, but he was smart.

"It's multiple sclerosis," Dr. Greenstein proffered his diagnosis. What an opening, and *what the fuck is multiple sclerosis?*

"You have seven lesions on your spine and five lesions in your head. I suggest a cycle of weekly intramuscular interferon injections (I will refer to this medication's brand name of Avonex going forward. Seriously, what the hell is interferon?), and we should start you on a prednisone drip to reduce the inflammation. I have taken the liberty for sending all the needed prescriptions to the pharmacy you provided us, and they should be ready by the time you get home. Any questions?"

He spoke to Steve but inclined the question of questions to us. Without knowing what to ask, we told the shrewd specialist we needed to take some time to process the situation. We were literally speechless. We committed to make contact regarding questions or more information as the needs arose.

Steve and I exited the surreal scene and headed to the train station for the trip home. We sat while we waited. We found our way to the station bar and sat in bewildered silence during our first beer.

"Is MS that thing that Jerry Lewis does the telethons for?" Steve inquired.

"Pretty sure that's muscular dystrophy, but I could be wrong."

"What's the difference?"

"How the hell should I know, we'll look it up when we get home, plus Greenstein gave a shit load of reading material."

We finished our beer and found the platform marked as our line home. We were headed into the unknown, all the while, Steve's immune system was dissolving the myelin sheath that surrounded and protected his nervous system. This was a tricky one. Sometimes this disease would hide dormant in the system and you'd never know you'd have it. Other research would compare it to Lou Gehrig's disease, leaving the one affected to a swift decline and an even swifter deterioration of the entire nervous system. This is also known as ALS. I didn't know what to think and resolved myself to just pay attention and go with the flow.

Steve worked full-time for a year after his diagnosis. As I mentioned, Steve's internal temperature always ran a little hot, and now, with the MS, it was all out of whack. Lowering his internal temperature was managed with the use of an ice vest to work that weighed over twenty pounds. In the mornings, I would pack twelve extra ice packs in a cooler and change them throughout the day. His right leg was getting worse and he would have mini-tumbles while at work.

His clients were growing increasingly concerned. Steve's condition was not going to allow him to keep up with his workload at the salon. His clients trusted me enough to take over in times of need, so I helped out with his client load.

It was a Tuesday morning in middle of August, almost a year to the day of his initial diagnosis. Getting out of the house was a struggle that morning, and I knew something was up. Steve was only two clients deep in his appointment book for the day when he told me that it was over. He could not work anymore. I did not realize what he was trying to tell me at that moment, but as he rose to finish his second client that morning, he fell flat on his face. I got it. Embarrassed, ashamed, and confused, we collected him and settled him on the sofa in the reception area. I had Valina (our receptionist) cancel the rest of our clients for the day. Steve's client understood what was transpiring, so I finished up her hair and took Steve home. Sitting at the dining room table over a couple of Bud Lights, he cried and simply said it was just too hard to work. He was losing strength in his hands and the nerve damage was really affecting his stand and walk normally.

Steve's mother, who moved in literally next door to be closer to Steve after his diagnosis, came over and immediately got on the phone to Social Security Disability, and together they completed the necessary forms as I was requesting Steve's file from his neurologist. The ball was literally in motion. We drank well that night as we discussed the possibilities, made a living will and advance directives, and then completed the dreaded will. He was always prepared for everything. This was no exception. I left Steve to his own devices the next morning, and for the first time in years, I drove to work alone. It was an incredibly odd feeling.

I contacted corporate that morning, informed them of Steve's further physical decline, and that he wouldn't be returning to work. I assured them we would do our best to keep his clients in house, but the choice was the clients'. We were able to retain almost 80 percent of his business. Corporate was satisfied, and the remaining staff were more than happy to have a bigger paycheck, circumstances notwithstanding. Steve is home alone all day now, while the world around him continued on. He loved his work, he was accustomed to a busy professional life, and I could see that staying at home was slowly driving him crazy. Steve being alone at home with his thoughts was rapidly spiraling downward in depression, anger, and frustration. Coming home at night was always a surprise. *What mood will he be in?* If he was drunk, it was going to be a long night. If he was in decent spirits, the conversation would generally digress into him voicing his feelings of uselessness.

In one year, he went from working full-time, to being essentially home-bound. He progressed from a cane to a walker. Then, from the walker he moved to a manual wheelchair. We eventually found ourselves in receipt of a snazzy new Jazzy, a power chair that could reach a speed of two miles an hour. We moved furniture to make the house more accessible. We swapped the glass surround in the bathroom for a shower curtain and a shower chair. During the evenings while watching TV, we brought out the commode so he wouldn't have to constantly get his chair stuck in the bathroom, and he could just pee in the living room while not missing a minute of his favorite shows. Medication upon medication followed. In addition to his weekly shot of Avonex, there was a bevy of painkillers, anti-anxiety medication, mineral replacements, and eventually a blood thinner. Steve was calling the salon more than usual one Saturday, complaining of a pain in his side when he took a deep breath. I ignored the first couple calls, knowing that I only had an hour to go before I could leave to be of service. Looming in my mind was Steve's higher-than-normal pain threshold. He was a person who could have a tooth removed without Novocain. Filled with dread, I called our neighbor across the street. She was an ER nurse. I hoped she would be home, and she was, thankfully. I would deal with the situation as best I could when I got home. She stayed with him until I got home, and she strongly suggested that we call an ambulance. Once it was decided, Mom and Jim came over, and we loaded Steve into the van. We headed to the hospital on a Saturday night for an emergency room visit. This was not going to be fun. The results indicated that he had a mini-stroke as a result of a pulmonary embolism or a cardiac thrombo-embolism. He was "throwing clots" as the white-coats would say, and a venous filter was needed to act as a blender of sorts, chopping up clots when they passed through his circulatory system. A daily Warfarin regimen was added to "thin" his blood out a little. One more pill each day …

The myriad tests had revealed that Steve a genetic mutation that affected his body's ability to keep blood clotting in check. He was advised by the doctor to contact his family and encourage them to get tested for the genetic mutation as well. It was hereditary and could cause similar problems in those that have the inherited gene, multiple sclerosis or not. Steve called his family and told those who did not know what happened, and suggested they get themselves tested for the mutation.

This was when medical science threw Steve's mother under the bus. Steve had a brother and two sisters, and Jim was husband number three. Jim did not father any of the children, and he did not have to be tested. So mother, brother, and two sisters go off to find out about their fate and genetic harmony. Steve's mother tested positive for the mutation. Steve's brother also tested positive for the mutation. One sister had positive results as well. The other sister tested negative. *Hmmmm ...* the whore was found out.

Steve's mother was clearly the carrier of the gene mutation so it made sense that all the children would test positive the same mutation. When Steve found out everyone's results, he was quick to put the pieces together. During Steve's mom's first marriage, and while she had two young boys, she had an extra-marital affair. Her husband at the time who we assumed was the father of all the kids, was in jail for attempted rape of a young girl who was hitch hiking down Route 95, according to Mother Dearest, and she became pregnant with sister number two. This was new information for all the kids. Mother had to come clean, very reluctantly, but she did. I think her loathing of Steve was exacerbated by this event. I, on the other hand, wanted to call the *Jerry Springer Show*. I really did think of calling. We could have used a vacation.

After the stroke, Steve was incredible at fending for himself a majority of the time I was away for work. Being home alone was certainly not in his favor though. He was visibly worn by the time I got home each day, and his deterioration had become more and more evident. He would call the salon every couple of hours, chitchat with Valina, and tie up the phones. If I was not there, or if I was with a client, and could not take his call, he would get pissy. "Where were you?" was a question I fielded a million times if once.

It was oppressing and exhausting to manage a million-dollar salon, manage the staff of said salon, manage said staff's benefits, keep our clients satisfied and returning regularly to said salon, keep up with corporate's financial information generated from said salon, make sure there are enough damn towels in said salon, and deal with someone at home who needs constant emotional, physical, and medical support.

My prayers were answered. I received word from my regional manager that she was coming down to talk with the staff "for a few minutes." This struck me as odd immediately. Her office was over two hours away, and this level of interaction with her was a complete break from her norm. This woman would call and tie me up endlessly on a busy Saturday, and in a salon, *every* Saturday is busy. The cow would eat into the phone while she parroted life-and-death information on how to break up the OPI nail-and-thong promo and sell the thongs for $5.99. *What warrants facetime in this woman's world?*

She was a dumpy, crumply, blonde-bob. She wore a pair of "these glasses make me look smart" glasses and had a cackle that was as piercing as it was nerve-wracking.

We all gathered in the reception area and she informed us that Elizabeth Arden will be shutting down the department store division in an attempt to focus on the free-standing locations. "But, don't fret," she offered all of us the chance to take our clients and join the staff at our Bala Cynwyd location, located in Saks Fifth Avenue, a department store. The irony of her offer will give you an aneurism if you think about it too long, just let it go.

We all sat motionless, stunned, and attention seemingly focused as she informed us of the exit strategy. No one listened. The salon was set to close in thirty days. When she was done, I asked the phone-chomper to step outside while I talked with my staff. This situation could have proven very lucrative. Being the forward-thinker that I am, now armed with a greater sense of business savvy, I suggested we approach one salon in the area, negotiate a signing bonus, and a week for the smoothest transition possible. Think of it, $500,000 a year walking through your business's door and literally setting up shop. It was an opportunity that any shop owner would kill for; we would only have to prove ourselves cohesive in the transition. The numbers spoke for themselves. My employees spoke for themselves as well, and hairdressers are prone to panic. All chose otherwise.

My panic set in when details of my life in America made it to the forefront of my "next-step" brainstorming. I was in America on a work visa that was conditional upon my employment with Arden. So, no Arden, no job. What a way to end the day. I stayed late that day, much to Steve's dismay, and copied all my client files. Relief visibly washed over Steve when I informed him of the day's events. That evening we planned. I sought guidance and clarity from my grapefruit Goose spirit drink.

Our plan was simple, we were going to carve out a space in our basement and play "salon." The challenge really was all my stranded clients and convincing them to come to our house for their routine beautification. Most of our clients were well aware of Steve's condition, and the situation was planned and sold to be more of a social engagement than simply going to a salon to have work done. We could encourage the gals to come in groups when possible. I could make a little nosh, serve a little vino, and everyone would leave satiated and looking great. It was going to work, and I could spend all day with Steve.

The regional blonde "cow" called a few days before the final closing date. She wanted numbers from the retail sales and to make sure I faxed her the weekly flash report before I left. "Oh, and make sure you package up all the remaining retail to send back to the warehouse," she added nonchalantly.

"Sure, I'll do everything except pack up the retail," was my retort.

"Michael, that's your job," she countered.

"Rub a lamp," was my parting advice. I was the last one to leave the salon the last day of business. I left her a classic shade to go with whatever lamp she found to pack up the retail products in the salon as well. Our layout there had eight doors providing access to all areas of the spa and salon, and for five years, no one had had a clue where the keys to all of them were hidden. During those five years the doors would be accidentally locked from time to time, and I had learned how to pick those locks in seconds. The big, blonde cow had not. So, I "accidentally" locked all eight doors that evening and locked the Arden glass door one last time on my way out. I dropped the key off with security and turned in my ID badge as I left the department store. Joe, one of our security guards, was on duty that night, and just so happened to be a client and friend from my tenure at the salon. He was aware of what was taking place with regard to our shut-down.

"Would you like this key to somehow go missing?" he probed.

"What key?" was my riposte.

The first few weeks at home with Steve were calm enough. He was able to transfer himself from chair to power chair, get his own tea, and fix lunch if he really got a hair up his ass. I was enjoying the absence of salon-drama-bullshit and became an avid fan of *Jerry Springer*, not my finest vice. I set up the salon and clients started reappearing. They would stop upstairs to say hi to Steve, I would take them down stairs to beautify them, and they would leave once all was said and done. Wash, rinse, repeat. The clients enjoyed it, and I loved not having to leave the house. Our plan was working.

During a calm day with nothing going on, he was still in bed by eight to watch his programs, take his evening meds, and eventually drift off. This left me with a lot of free time to surf Facebook, YouTube, and research more and more about this new roommate named multiple sclerosis. As I read more or more on the disease, I became more and more terrified of it. The range of severity and aggressiveness of the disease ranged from mild and almost undetectable to full-blown "secondary progressive," very aggressively and rapidly attacking the myelin sheath. Steve's continual regimen of MRIs confirmed the latter in his case.

One day, a friend, Antthony, sent me an email telling me to check him out on some internet radio show called *At Home with Victoria*. Ever adventurous, that evening I made sure Steve was all settled in bed before I tuned in to Antthony on this radio show. I prepared myself a red Solo cup of chardonnay with a couple ice cubes because I am classy like that, logged on to the show's website, took note of the chat room, and readied myself for the show.

The topic for this airing was, "Entrepreneurship and What It Takes," and it was surprisingly well-produced and professional. I was active in the chat room and found it most flattering when the host,

Victoria, would mention my name and ask Antthony my questions. Equally gratifying was hearing Antthony acknowledge that I was a friend as he gave the audience his answer.

I am snooper, so I did some digging in to this Victoria persona. She was a news journalist who was mentored by Dan Rather. She had worked for several TV stations and eventually became the morning gal at WMAR. In essence, she was an African American Diane Sawyer with a great smile and a great voice.

Steve was happy to indulge me with an hour of internet radio time, and I continued to tune in week after week every Thursday at 8:00 p.m. I was active in the chat room and eventually developed friendships with the other regulars. When shows were announced, we would quickly share it on Facebook, etc. It was a new digital social scene. I was in. Victoria took note of me and used several of my questions during her interviews. One evening, I had hair clients scheduled late, and I had to miss my date with Victoria. I waved my clients good-bye at 10:00 p.m. that evening. Steve was calmly sleeping by this time of night, so I made ready the ever-classy solo cup and opened my email. I was shocked. I had message from Victoria herself. "Where were you tonight?" she queried.

"I had clients, how was the show?" This seemed odd, but I was intrigued at the interest.

"Five people emailed me and asked me where you were," she responded quickly.

"How kind," I replied, at a bit of a loss for words.

I did not think much of it at the time, but I was honestly flattered that I was missed, if only by my fellow audience members.

The weeks went on, and Steve and I had a good rhythm going. He was still able enough to move around the house at the time, but the limitations were increasing. On the upside of that downer, was tuning in for Victoria's show and my chat room discussions each week. *At Home with Victoria* had become my weekly look-forward-to event. Understandably enough, I had to miss another show in conflict with a late in the evening scheduling. I loved my Thursday evenings, but the paying public came first. I received another communiqué from Victoria that evening.

"When you have a few minutes, give me a call." She had given me her <u>home</u> phone number.

Giving her number to me was surprising enough, but when I dialed, she actually picked up. I was floored.

"Hey, you, where were you tonight?" she asked as she had when I last missed her show.

"I had clients again, gotta bring home the bacon here." Indeed. I managed to use the word *bacon* in my first spoken sentence with Victoria.

"Well, I received over thirty emails, again asking where Michael was. So, this is my offer. Would you be willing to become chat room producer?" She left the proposition hanging for my response.

"Not really sure what that is, but why not?" I responded completely baffled. The duties of chat room producer entailed disseminating website addresses from the guests, sharing links to guests' products online, and all while making the other chat room users feel comfortable and welcome. I would throw out a couple jokes, just being myself. All while, refilling my red solo cup as so desired, and I could do everything clad in a bathrobe from my kitchen table. It was a new outlet and a sweet gig. It made my mind work and I met some really fascinating people. During my nights of insomnia, I would search YouTube for the newest in music, dance, and independent film. Some of the stuff I was watching was spectacular and worthy of sharing, but I was still green in my role with the show. I did not want to overstep the bounds of my role for the show or Victoria, but I was not getting paid so she could not fire me. I took a risk.

In the wake of that one risk, Victoria and I went on to do over 370 shows together. I was her Entertainment Co-Host and producer on the *Blog Talk Radio Network*. Our show is still available as a free download on iTunes. Together, we elevated the show and were fortunate to have guests such as international fashion photographer, Mike Ruiz; Genie Francis revealed her cocaine addiction during the Luke and Laura years; the Fonz, Henry Winkler, even gave us an hour of his time. I was able to introduce the listeners of *At Home with Victoria* to the indie film and music arena. I had established a rapport with the niche of directors, producers, actors, singers, and writers.

The whole collection of artists enjoyed being on the show, and we grew to be known by many up-and-comers who were integrating veteran actors into their little indie attempts. It was exciting, and I loved every minute of it. In a way, Victoria rescued me.

After a year on the show, my new professional network was growing. The year was full of making connections and highlighting some of the best new talent. I was then confident enough to attempt some big boy shit. I forced myself to ask to be on the red carpet at the Indie Soap Awards in New York.

Request granted.

I was beyond animated as I gathered myself for the project. We went by rail from Wilmington to NYC. I arrived in New York around noon, and I immediately checked on Steve. I was feeling guilty for letting my focus drift from him, and was worried. He was at that time still able to get around and fend for himself. Plus, his mother and Jim were right next door. Anything that needed immediate attention, they could handle it. I had to conduct some pre-interviews for bumpers to include in the video that was to be edited and back online within twenty-four hours after the awards show. *I was only going to be gone twenty-four hours.*

We checked into the Holiday Inn off 59th, right in the heart of Hell's Kitchen. I phoned home to check on Steve. He answered the phone frantically crying. Mother had come over to check on him, and during her visit, she claimed that Steve molested his younger sister years ago. She suggested that before he died, he should acknowledge it and make amends for his actions. Steve had launched into a state of rage and kicked her out of the house. I calmed him down and assured him that his mother was a total asshole, and I would deal with it when I got home.

Honestly, Steve did have a temper, but it was usually only spurned by someone challenging him or questioning him. I bore witness to his rage more than once and endured a couple of bloody nights as a punching bag. His practice of making someone understand turned violent many times. I really never thought I would take more than I could, but I did. It made me a stronger person. Regardless of Steve's temper, her indictment and declaration were not the subject matter that needed to be broached with a man in his condition and general state of agitation.

I did the pre-interviews. I was last on the red carpet, right behind a sassy and comical blonde gal by the name of Erin Brown. She was from Los Angeles, and she had a hilarious show on YouTube called *Hot on the Red Carpet*. She was astute with a twisted mind wrapped in curiosity and sugar. I had watched all her stuff and adored her. Brad and I made it back to the hotel around midnight, and we edited till 8:00 a.m. the next morning. Brad was my camera man for the event. He was a young man with a wicked photographic eye and happened to be Steve's nephew. We uploaded our edited footage and were the first ones with edited coverage of the award ceremony. I treated Brad to some good eggs Benedict in true New York diner style. Our trek home was scheduled at 10:00 a.m., I was anxious to see and learn what really went down at the home front. Jim, Steve's stepfather, picked me up at the train station in Wilmington. Brad's mother picked him up.

In the van back home, Jim said to me, "Well, that was a quick trip. I thought you were coming back tomorrow."

"That was the plan but when I called Steve he told me about the visit with mother. What happened?" We were cautiously feeling out each other's conversational comfort zone boundaries.

"I'm not really sure, but all I know is that Steve kicked her out of the house and told her never to come back." He was totally detached from the words he spoke. "Why did he say that?" I pushed for more. "I have no idea." I could smell *it* on his words.

*It* smelled like the rules in my family, and the division lines were clearly drawn. Either, you were Team Mother, or you were on Team Steve. Jim was clearly Team Mother. Not a surprise, but I was suspicious of him not knowing anything. I walked into the house and was greeted with a total mess. Things were knocked over, an element on the stove was on, spilled tea was everywhere, chairs were shoved about, and Steve was in his room sobbing. After physically calming him down, I made a fresh cup of tea for the each of us. Once he was settled in his power chair, and once he caught his breath, we began to talk. Steve said his mother came over shortly after I left to check on him. As they talked, she shifted the conversation to Steve's alleged molestation of his younger sister, now a three-time prisoner, heroin addict, alcoholic, user, and manipulator. She was the addict that was difficult to have any sympathy for whatsoever. Mother thought she was always the smartest one. I listened while my blood boiled. Mother comes to our home and stirs up a shit storm, and I got to come home to deal with the aftermath. Fun. My hatred for Mother was ever snowballing. For those of you who have ever been a caregiver or a family member who is taking care of someone with secondary progressive multiple sclerosis, I applaud you. People enduring this disease are treated to episodes called exacerbations. Usually spurned on by excessive heat, medication imbalance, and stressful situations, an exacerbation is when the nerve endings are inflamed causing, basically, a short circuit in the brain directly affecting mobility, cognitive reasoning, and response. The treatment is a round of prednisone drips that could be administered intravenously at home. They would give Steve a PICC line, and it was up to me to flush the lines after administering the drips. The treatment stretched over five days, and Steve would receive a drip bag every twelve hours. During these treatments was when Steve would be at his best. His vision was better, his mobility was better, and he was full of piss and vinegar. Good times!

Then, we would have to taper him off over ten days, weaning him off the drip. The prednisone reduces inflammation around the nerve core, it is a steroid. Once the drip ends, the body realizes it has to compensate for the shift in hormone levels and caused extreme irritability, frustration, and depression. We endured fourteen of these exacerbations over a four-year period. His condition progressed to the point of Steve being bedridden. His muscles had atrophied to the point where it was impossible for him to put shoes on. He would choke while he ate so we had to feed him spoon-by-spoon. Steve was a proud man and this drove him crazy. His bodily functions were not registering with his senses anymore, and the lesions on his spine left him with little feeling below his abdomen. Some nights we would change the bed three times. He did not know when he was urinating. Again, with all the medication, voiding his bowels became the main focus. Showers were every other day with a whore's bath in between. We would wheel into the shower and transfer him to the shower seat. He was able to shower himself, wash his own hair, shave, and restore some of his dignity while I quickly changed the bed sheets. Then, he would call me in for the back wash. I would wash his back, then take the head off the shower and use the hose to facilitate a water enema. This worked almost every time. We would flush the nasty out of him. I would scoop the void out of the tub and gingerly drop it in the appropriate vessel. We would finish up, get him clothed, and transferred back to his chair. Then on to the hospital bed and I would tuck him in until the next need arose. I would comb his hair, put some fancy stink on him, and the afternoon was complete. This continued for four years.

Being a full-time caregiver to your lover crosses so many boundaries. The once sexual body you used to caress in passing, or in the throes of passion, is replaced by a new facade declaring that the body you once lusted after was now only some vessel housing internal organs that have daily functions. The entire house worked around the multiple sclerosis's schedule.

I spent five years sleeping on the sofa because the acoustics in our house deemed that spot my safe zone. It was the only space where I could hear every noise he made. I was always ready to go at any minute. Till this day, my training during this time honed my hearing to the keenness of being able to hear an ant fart from across the street. Eventually, we got to the point where I had to involve hospice. I could not care for Steve on my own. Delaware hospice was a life saver and a logical sounding board for what was about to happen. For the next year and a half, all Steve's medications were covered by them; I had a social worker who came out to the house twice a week; nurses would come check on him every other day to ensure there were no bed sores and to confirm my level of care. Someone could even come out to give me an hour a week out of the house. I used that free time to go to the grocery store to pick up meds and groceries for the upcoming week.

In Steve's final months, we were at one of our scheduled six weeks visit with his neurologist, a short man with a short man attitude. His toupee was cheaper than his shoes, and indicated where his priorities lay. We informed him of the latest exacerbation, and he looked at us like he was hearing this for the first time. Steve and I indicated that the drip was no longer as effective as it once was, and we inquired if there was an alternative that may be up for consideration. He assured us that the best treatment was for Steve to go through *another* round of prednisone but at a higher concentration. This was the game changer. Steve and I had discussed the eventuality of his condition. We had been working on accepting the terms of his condition since diagnosis. No more meds. It was time to let nature take its course. "We've chosen to go off all medications except for those needed for pain. Steve is a DNR and has chosen to donate his body to the University of Delaware to further aid in the research and development of this disease." They were long-dreaded words finally spoken.

He looked at us dumbfounded. The tiny man, in his tiny suit, had his little mind blown. "Why would you do that?" He asked quite surprised at the change of course.

"Look, we all know there's no cure for this and until stem cells are approved by the FDA, there's really no chance that Steve's progression will halt. Steve and I are both okay with this decision."

"I'm done, I can't take another pill or be poked again. I just want to relax and go home." It was Steve's acquiescence to what lay ahead.

The little man in the little suit accepted what he heard and lead us out of his office. "Let's book one for Steve three months from now," he prompted.

"I'll call you if I need you, let's try it that way," was Steve's counter. We were having a cigarette, processing what we just declared, during the wait for ParaTransit to shuttle us home. Once home, we laughed and ripped that little man in the little suit with the tiny mind a brand-new asshole. We would figure this out. We were both strong and capable. In the harshness of tomorrow's unavoidable realities, we both knew different, but tonight, we knew everything by accepting everything. With hospice now a part of our lives, and I, now armed with the Victoria the news lady teachings, we decided to document the end stages of one with multiple sclerosis. The web series was called *Tales from the Crip*. Steve chose the title. Each week we would record our accounts of what happened the week prior. We filmed and released thirty-two episodes, including our wedding. Steve was in the bed and I by his side. We had a studio audience during some episodes, and we had special guests from time to time. Actors, singers, and the like that I interviewed on the radio in days past would stop by and chat with Steve. Generally, when hospice is recommended, assessed, approved, and put in motion, it's fair to assume that days are numbered. Steve's case was a little different. He was under hospice care for a year, he just kept hanging on. Dying at forty-eight years old was what seriously pissed him off, and *Tales from the Crypt* was a great outlet to bleed that energy off. We did one show with actress Dee Freeman that evolved from lighthearted fun into revealing questions that shocked Steve into facing his situation head on. He knew he was dying, but there's always that part of one's constitution that still holds on to hope. The ilk of hope that eases an individual to sleep with dreams of waking in the morning to learn that what is was just a nightmare. The truthful disappointment returned every morning like clockwork.

The last major event before his passing involved the blood thinners was prescribed for his clotting disorder. He was too weak to be transported to LabCorp for his PT and INR to be tested. PT or Prothrombin-Time and INR or International Normalized Ratio are assays evaluating the extrinsic pathway of coagulation. These tests determine the clotting tendency of the blood, in the measure of warfarin dosage, liver damage, and vitamin K status. The normal range is between 2 and 3.

I tried to manage the daily dosage of warfarin with two major factors to assess. I had to know everything he ate that day, and I had to keep a constant tally of his alertness, responsiveness, and movements throughout the day.

One day, he was particularly pale and could not keep anything down. I called Mother and we decided to call the ambulance.

With accurate dosing of warfarin, the clotting factor should be between 2 and 3, as I mentioned. Steve was at 13. This meant that his blood was so resistant to coagulation that it was causing issues with the oxygenation of his red blood cells, and his heart rate was racing to compensate for the imbalance. Steve laid there, laboring on oxygen. The doctor started an aggressive detox, if you will, using vitamin K, Mother Nature's coagulant. During all the confusion, the doctor on duty handling Steve's case pulled me aside. "Does Steve have a living will and advance directives?"

My response was cautious. "Yes, there should be a copy on file with Christiana Hospital."

I could see the fallaciousness of my response on his face. "Well, we can't seem to locate it. Can you bring the copies to me?" "Sure," I said, "I'll bring them by in the morning." I was trying my best not to focus on what the doctor's urgency was regarding the paperwork. "We don't have that kind of time. Do you know if he has a DNR or not?"

My brain exploded with the realization of his urgency. *The* urgency became very real all of a sudden.

"Yes, I'll go get them now." I scramble out.

I walked out to see Mom and Jim standing and waiting for information.

"Jim, can you take me home. The doctor needs some paperwork sooner than later."

Jim and I headed home post haste, I retrieved the needed papers, and we returned to the hospital to deliver what was needed. I handed the documents over, and the doctor asked, "Are you power of attorney or is his mother or another family member?"

"I am," I marshalled.

"Okay, then I need to talk to you." Those were not words I wanted to hear. "The fact of the matter is his elevated levels. We are trying to get his oxygen levels up, the vitamin K shots will certainly expedite this process, but the results have to be monitored continuously, and Steve cannot be without proper oxygen. He will benefit from physical and speech therapy, which our people are lining up for you now in our Wilmington location. Honestly, we don't know what level of Steve you will be taking home. He'll be with us for at least a week so we can monitor his levels and assess the level of deterioration. Time will tell."

I wanted to punch him in the throat. Yet I appreciated him leveling with me. Steve was moved to the ICU and was aware enough to express his need for a cigarette; with my denial came his stream of profanities. I apologized to the nurse for Steve's behavior. Then came one of the most leveling statements ever made by a human being. It still resonates in my head to this very day.

"You have to remember, he's sick."

*Yeah, I forgot that little truth.* I managed to keep my words to myself.

With Steve now settled in ICU, I knew he was in good hands. I caught a cab home to take a nap.

Once he was stable, Steve was moved to a rehab facility. He spent six weeks doing strength training, speech therapy, dexterity therapy, and eventually became the asshole he was before the incident. Hospice was up to snuff on the information and little changes were made.

One of the best things about being in the hospice network for me was respite care. Every six months, Steve would go into a care facility so the caregiver (me) could have a break. I had three five-day stretches off during our collective time with hospice. The first time was great. Steve thought of it as summer camp. He made friends, ate in the cafeteria, played games, and had a good time. The second visit was much like the first, but he was left alone a lot this time which gave him time to think and question his mortality. The third time was a mess. His dementia had progressed to hallucinations and irrationality. He must have called home thirty-nine times the first day. He would be crying and begging to come home. I, in turn, was overcome with guilt and frustration. The staff took it upon themselves to take over and allow only one call a day, which fueled his frustration. All three respite trips I spent sleeping as much as possible. Sleeping in a quiet house with my cat, watching reruns of *Roseanne*, *Will and Grace*, and *Friends*. No news.

This last trip for Steve would really be his last trip.

He returned home after his last five-day vacation to a new airflow mattress to alleviate pressure sores. We had finally healed the one on his tailbone, and no one wanted to repeat that week-long process. Of course, the mattress and Steve arrived at the same time. We placed him in his chair and waited for the mattress to be filled with air. When all was complete, I was convinced Steve had soiled himself in some manner. I wheeled Steve into the bedroom to clean him up only to reveal three more pressure sores. I cleaned him from his accident and dressed the wounds. I put him in clean clothes and made him some tea. He indulged with a couple of tokes of pot and started to calm down. Our friend Susie had come over to spend the night. I felt I needed someone to be there to sit with Steve while I went over the notes from the rest home.

We dined on grilled salmon, asparagus, and fried green tomatoes. Susie fed him; his hands were that deteriorated from atrophy. With dinner finished, and all the commotion of the day behind us, Steve, looking all flushed, told me, "I want to go outside tomorrow."

"Sure, we will go down and sit by the pool, maybe get some good vitamin D." It was an encouraging notion for the both of us.

I took his tray, filled up his sippy-cup, and cleaned the kitchen. By the time I made it back to the bedroom, Steve had already fallen asleep.

Susie and I watched *American Idol* quietly, making sure he would not be disturbed.

Steve died the following morning, August 28, at 7:28 a.m. I woke up to relieve myself that morning, checked on Steve, and saw him sleeping with his mouth open—he usually did. As I sat, *yes*, I sit to pee, I would usually hear a big gasp for air intermittently. I wasn't hearing it this morning. I flushed and walked into his bedroom. His body was warm, but I could not find his pulse. I tried to wake him. I pressed down on his diaphragm and Steve's last breath floated through morning stillness. I taped his eyelids down; Steve was an eye donor. I woke little Susie, and I called hospice. The house became a confusion of people in motion with all end points leading to Steve being placed on a gurney and taken away from me.

I sent Steve's brother to tell Mother of the news. His mother, who had never returned to see her son for two years as he withered away in his bed, and her husband, barged through our front door soon after. Mother and Jim walked in past the hospice staff, paid no mind to anyone honestly, looked at Steve, and stormed right back out. During her exit, Mother yelled, "See, he's not even crying." Obviously, taking a shot at me.

Mind you, I never saw a tear eke from that narrow-minded, over highlighted, hypocritical bigot's eyes, but I digress.

I looked out the window as they loaded Steve in the back of an SUV. I don't know what I was expecting, but I thought they sent a hearse or something more official. I guess I was wrong.

The house quieted down, and since my friends Kelly and Susie were here for it all; I suggested we all get out of the house for lunch. We went to Harry's Savoy Grill on the waterfront in Wilmington. We bellied up to the bar. I had a double dirty martini, Kelly had a margarita, and Susie had a diet Coke. The menu was a blur, and I was feeling a little dizzy. The effort to make small talk at the time was more work than I was willing to exert, and with the cacophony associated with any given bar, everyone's voices sounded muddled. It was like listening to music or someone trying to talk to you while you are under water. By the time the food came, I was ready to go home. I felt the need to be enclosed and not so exposed. I felt raw, like a bad sunburn in the summer. We took our lunch to go and headed home, after we hit the liquor store.

I shared a few glasses of chardonnay with the gals on the back deck, overlooking the pool. Sitting in the afternoon sun of fall was exactly what I needed. We reminisced together through stories we had about Steve. It was nice.

The gals left early evening, and I sat, glass in hand, in a very quiet house. The gravity of the situation slowly seeped in. Logically, I was sound. Emotionally, I wasn't sure. There was a part of me that wasn't surprised.

Later that evening, and half in the bag, I entered the death room. I made the bed with proper sheets sans the drip pad and three towels, lowered the head of the bed, took off the guard rails, and pushed it against the wall. *It looked like a perfectly comfortable day bed.* I packed up all the diapers, wet wipes, alcohol pads, the hospital tray, and pushed the snazzy Jazzy into the closet. I swept and washed the floor, cleaned up urine that I missed, and found a few pills that Steve must have dropped at some point in time. I took down the curtains. They were sticky with tar and nicotine; Steve was a smoker right up to the end. He was no quitter. I opened the sliding patio doors and let the fresh air filter in and condition whatever energy was lingering.

The surreal nature of the entire saga was flooding my mind. Steve was bed-bound for the last four years of his life. I slept on the sofa for the last four years of our life together. "Michael!" He would yell to let me know that either he needed water, cigarettes, a painkiller, or as a call to arms during the dreaded wet-the-bed nights. He did find relief, but when you take enough pain meds to power down a thoroughbred, he would sleep right through urination. He did sleep with the urinal already in anticipation, but that was not the most effective remedy. One night, I changed those sheets, cleaned up, and changed Steve five times. Would I grow to miss those times?

The afternoon after Steve left the house on his final voyage, the guy from hospice stopped by to go over some details. We discussed the obituary; he confirmed Steve's wishes to have his body donated to science; that he arrived at the University of Delaware safe and sound; did I want an urn, you know … those kinds of questions and issues. During this, the mother next door opens her kitchen window and screen, pokes her head out, and shouts, "I'm going to demand an autopsy. I want to know what drugs Steve had in his system because I think *he* (meaning me) killed my son. I'm going to sell that house out right from under him."

"Get back in the kitchen, Carol. This doesn't concern you anymore," I snapped back to her.

"Of course, it concerns me, I'm his mother."

"Well, if it concerned you so much, how come you didn't come over and see your son for the last three years?" I answer sharply.

"It's only been two," was her only response.

He could see what I was dealing with. "Look, this nice man will come over to your house after he leaves here. He will gladly fill you in and answer any questions you have. Now, please leave us alone."

She slammed the window and walked from view away. I gave the guy a little back story regarding her the familial situation, we finished what we needed to cover, and I apologized for throwing him to the wolf next door.

As he was leaving, I asked if he would call me after his meeting with the head in the window. He agreed, and we laughed.

He was over there for about an hour before I saw him exit the lion's den. I watched as he pulled away and eagerly awaited his call. Ten minutes later, the phone rang. It was him, "I would have called you earlier, but I was afraid that your mother-in-law may be looking out the window at me." More laughter. "Boy, you really don't have a next-door friend, that's for sure. She did not speak well of you at all, but I was able to give her the information she needed and she started to calm down. Good luck dealing with her."

"Thank you so much for your patience and yes, I'm certainly not the favorite one. I will gladly heed your warning. Chat soon." So, this confirmed it. I wasn't overreacting. I wasn't crazy. She was.

I spent another two years sleeping on the sofa. Partly because I could not sleep in the other room, and partly because I had properly broken-in the sofa. It was one of the most comfortable places to be. My cat was my only roommate now. Chia was a red-white-and-black calico, quite rotund and very sassy. During Steve's illness, Chia acted more like a golden retriever, always by his side or laying between his legs. She did the same for me, but for me her favorite place was laying on my pillow, sharing it with my head. I continued to bring in clients and was still doing the radio show. I was staying busy, but on the days that I had nothing scheduled, I was much too happy to just lie on the sofa with my cat and watch reruns of *Friends*, *Roseanne*, and *Will and Grace*. Not one speck of news except for the dribs and drabs that made its way on the Facebook feed.

I dined simply on microwavable edibles and quickly discovered which ones were the best ones for the dollar. In three minutes, I could have a single serving gourmet meal at the ready. My depression cure-all had returned, and I was more than happy to welcome it. My entire life, my growing up years, my teen years, my hair school years, even then, alcohol never let me down. It washed my concerns away only to have them return the next day. It was a viciously destructive cycle. I see that now as I look back. I alienated the gals and most other friends, trusting only my cat and the lock on the door. I did not answer the phone. My only outings included walking the two miles to the grocery store. It was in the same market square where I could get my Franzia Chardonnay, cigarettes, and my favorite single-serving cuisine. The nights were the worst. While everyone else was sleeping, my mind began to race and I would spin scenes with Steve that I could have done different, or that I should have done. Before I knew it, I could see the sun peeking through the backyard bamboo.

Naps were the norm. I was thankful that I would tire my mind enough to have it just sort of stop, if only for a few hours. I had all Steve's leftover meds, his painkillers, and some gabapentin. A couple painkillers with a few glasses of wine usually sealed the deal regarding sleep. I was very *Valley of the Dolls,* without the fame and fortune. He had some morphine in IV form, but I never did try it. I had seen too many episodes of *Intervention*, not a really glamorous drug by any means. So, *yes*, during those two years, I was walking a slippery slope.

Steve died in August so everyone was thinking of the upcoming holiday season. I dreaded it. I had Thanksgiving, Christmas, and his birthday to get through.

For Thanksgiving, yes, the gals all invited me to their respective houses for the pagan holiday. Kelly had three kids, all under the age of thirteen … that was a definite no. Susie had fourteen dogs ranging in size from a squirrel to a horse; although I loved dogs, I did not feel up to fighting for my food. So I ordered the Bob Evans Thanksgiving feast for twenty-nine dollars. It included turkey, potatoes, stuffing, mac and cheese, turkey gravy, cranberries, and rolls. I did not have to share, and I did not have to dress up. Perfect. It was touted as a feast for four, but I had to call bullshit. It was a feast for four if each of you ate from tea cup saucers. Yet, it was the best turkey gravy *ever*.

Christmas was the same situation, different decorations. "Come on over! We're eating at three." I politely declined, outlining my need to start my own traditions, if only for myself at the time. I chose not watch my go-to faves like *Miracle on 42nd Street, National Lampoons Christmas Vacation,* or *Xanadu,* a weird choice, but just as believable as *Miracle*. Instead, for my viewing pleasure I chose *Ted, Carrie,* and still one of my favorite films to rewatch, *Postcards from the Edge*. I dined on a Swanson's fried chicken dinner with corn, instant potatoes, and that crappy brownie that always gets as hard as a hockey puck. With the cat on my feet, I pigged out and stopped only to wipe the chicken grease from my cheek and nurse on my red solo cup contents.

I had gained about eighty pounds I did not even notice. I was reflecting on the imagery my brain took in on a regular basis donned as I made a trip to the restroom to pee. I sat, now noticing that my belly was eclipsing the penis that I was once so proud of having. Now, I could only shave my balls if I had three mirrors on the floor, allowing me a most undesirable view. I used to be fit and thin, and I used to give a shit about what I looked like. Now, the only clothes I wore were the ones stain resistant to cream sauces and tears.

Something had to be done. I needed to check myself.

Radio made my voice look thin, that was a good thing, and it was the best form of a foundation I had going. Money was still coming in and Steve was smart enough to leave me some cha-ching, so that was off my head. I scrubbed the house from top to bottom and meditating on what I could do to maintain, restore, and reenter the world of normalcy.

My gal pal had just left her husband and was seeing a new guy. Since her husband had the kids on the weekend and she was living with her mother, she and her new beau needed a place on the weekends and hotel bills were really adding up. They offered $400 a month to stay the weekends. They would arrive on Friday and leave late Sunday afternoon. They kept to themselves mostly, or spent time going out, so it wasn't an imposition, and I enjoyed having them around. Extra money coming in ... check!

I started walking again. I ran when I was in high school and excelled at track, largely because I had to run away from the torch-wielding villagers that did not take kindly to people of my tribe. The weight was coming off ... check!

My depression wasn't really going away, but I did find a way to put it in a place. I was not going to let it dominate every aspect of my life.

I started doing more remote reporting with Victoria, and she soon became a close friend. I could trust her enough to let my guard down and show my weaknesses, one thing I wasn't very good at. We had fun and were able to cultivate our little niche on internet radio to attract some of the movers and shakers in Washington DC. Although I was overweight, I still had enough skills to scrub-up and show-off from time to time.

The minutia was settling into what was now my new normal, and I faced the truth. I was now an older gay man, a little bruised, with a little baggage. *Who would want to deal with that?* At the time, many people were getting on E-Harmony, Christian Mingle, and other dating sites, each one claiming such outstanding results with regards to helping you find "the right one for you."

Have you *seen* the amount of paperwork you have to fill out for E-Harmony account? Seriously, who has that kind of time? Then, the monthly fees, even then, were more than stupid to me. Obviously, there was no chance of me trying Christian Mingle. I was not feeling the possibility of being struck by lightning, and I could not hold out for the yet to be known advent of Farmers Only.

So, I found Plenty of Fish. It was free and when I scrolled down through the profiles, I soon discovered why. I took a leap of faith and met with couple people on the site. One was a guy named Steve (I will refer to him as Steve 2 from this point on). I thought, ugh, of all the luck. We met online and chatted several times on the phone. He seemed normal enough; he was working in finance and lived in Philadelphia. He lived on one of those narrow side streets where the address included a ½ or a ¼. For example, his address was 243 ¼ Logan Street. Cabs wouldn't even go down these streets. They were too narrow and had nowhere to go should another car come down the opposite way.

It was time for us to meet in the real world, and I was expected at his house around 7:00 p.m. The cab dropped me off on the corner of the block and told me, "Just walk on down, the house would be on the right-hand side." Thankfully, in an attempt to look cute, I was wearing leather soled shoes, perfect for a walk in two feet of snow. I knocked on the door and Steve 2 answered. Well, half of Steve 2 answered the door. He was 5'4, known to the gay world as a "pocket gay." The evening was not predicated on height, but *had I missed that on his profile?* Regardless, while one the phone one evening, he told me he was "In the middle of a move, so the house was in a state of organized disarray." I asked if there was anything he needed for his new house. "New underwear," was his answer. Being the asshole I am, that is what I got him. I offered my gifts, a six-pack of Hanes, and a copy of *The Prophet* by Kahil Gibran, in the hope that he would see the humor. He did.

Our evening together was enjoyable. We took a cab to this diner on Walnut Street. Old-school style with a great menu. The company was great, and the food was great. As we dined and conversed, I was mentally going over my checklist: he had a great smile, endearing blue eyes, balanced gray hair, he was a smoker, and he enjoyed a strong cocktail. I needed to look no further; I had hit the mother lode. We kissed modestly as our evening together came to a close, and I caught a cab to the train station from the diner.

While on the train home, he texted me about how much fun he had and wanted to do it again. My self-confidence soared.

He had a week off for his move coming up soon so we planned a day date. I took the train to Philadelphia early and got a good haircut. I had been hacking at it myself for a few years, I had to splurge. I treated myself to a light lunch of escargot in garlic, hazelnut butter at La Patisserie, overlooking Rittenhouse Square. I truly had a delightful day drinking in the city.

I was to meet Steve 2 at 3:00 p.m. at the Elephant and Castle, an English pub serving authentic English fare. Steve 2 entered as I was guzzling my second beer. He was giddy over our second meeting. I was flattered.

Turns out, Steve 2's giddiness had nothing to do with me. He was thrilled that he had been accepted to live in this exclusive building for senior gays and senior gay-friendly fag hags and lesbians. Apparently, it was very posh, and they had rooftop pot lucks on Friday nights. Bingo was Tuesdays.

He shared his good news with me and apologized ahead of time for having to call a couple of his friends to let them know of his good luck.

I understood completely. How exciting it must have been to have a full number on your new door.

He kept his promise and was continually checking his messages and taking congratulatory calls. I patiently sipped my beer and waited to be recognized as another person in the world.

We finished up at the Elephant and made our way to another restaurant, this one was on Spruce Street. While walking the downtown streets I was admiring the architecture of the buildings. They were truly stunning. "These buildings have some of the most interesting fack-aids," he declared.

"I beg your pardon, what did you say?" I was wondering if I had heard him correctly?

"The fack-aids, the fack-aids! Look up, see the top of that column, that's called a fack-ade!" he sternly informed me.

"Oh, is that what you call them here in America. In Canada, it's pronounced façade, fa-sahd." That was red flag number one. Did I mention that he had a master's degree?

We arrived at Finnegans restaurant. We were seated and we ordered a couple beers. Our drinks arrived and the waitress un-capped each beer at the table, placing each bottle before us. He took his napkin and violated the neck of his Bud Light bottle. I know some people like to wipe down the top of a soda can, but this guy was really going to town to ensure that no germs were to enter his little body. We both ordered cheeseburgers and fries, the house specialty. To give him credit, he did make it abundantly clear that he did not want a pickle. Not to even wave a pickle over the plate or to place the hamburger even close to the jar where the pickles taunted him. I found the request a little too vehement, but who was I to judge? He may have had a life threatening, harrowing experience by a pickle. I did not know all the facts. I was taking notes nonetheless.

We continued with light chitchat mainly on the topic of the new place he was sooo excited to move into. I listened and calmly waited for my cheeseburger and fries. The waitress returned and served us our meal. She sets mine down and it looked delicious! She places Steve 2's plate down and dun, dun, duuun … there it is, the dreaded pickle. The lovely girl who makes $2.10 an hour and lives off tips walks away. Steve 2 looks at me with a look of absolute disgust on his tiny little face.

"See! No one listens anymore!" he exclaims.

I reached over, grabbed the pickle, and quickly make the green bandit disappear. He frantically wipes his plate where the pickle made contact to make sure none of the pickle juice would touch the bun for his burger. He discarded the fries closest to the crime scene. Red flag number two went up.

We finished up and walked a block and a half to L BAR, a tiny hole-in-the-wall bar where happy hour is from noon until midnight. Taking both foibles in stride, I ordered a double dirty martini and prayed for a fast track to inebriation. We chatted throughout his phone continuing to chime notifications for this and that incoming communication. This continued for three martinis. I was privately contemplating catching a much earlier train home than I originally intended because I was starting to get miffed. He reported that he had to go to the washroom, and I excused myself to have a cigarette outside. I was watching the passers-by and enjoying the lung filling smoke as I turned to watch him exiting the bathroom and returning to our place at the bar. I had not noticed it before now; we were always in a jacket or dim lighting up to this point. This guy had no shoulders whatsoever. His form was reminiscent of the only wire hanger you were sometimes forced to use when you hand-washed a heavy cardigan with Woolite, wrung out most of the moisture, and made do with said wire hanger. You know how the heavy sweater contorts the hanger and the hanger bends forming an inverted *U* shape? I got a naked mental picture and shuddered. I didn't think shoulder pads would come close to helping this one. There was red flag number three.

I slugged down my martini and in a not-so-polite manner, dismissed myself, claiming I had some business to attend that I could not readily explain right then and there. I caught the next train home.

Reflecting on my evening as I was conveyed home, I giggled out loud. A week must have passed before he called and said he had to break it off with me. I was too needy, and right now he just needed to have fun. I agreed fully. I had dodged a bullet.

The other guy I met was named John; he was a bartender at a place the gals and I graced once in a while called Tailgates. It was a bar where time stood still for the year 1989. The clothes, the hair, the line-dancing all left plenty to be desired, but the prices were good and you did not have to pay for entertainment.

We agreed to meet at the Texas Roadhouse right down from my house. It was election day as I recall, and John was coming directly from the polls. He arrived, and he had a fun smile that made him look a little special in the head. He possessed a confident walk and a nice ass. He had always been kind, affable, and funny while tending bar for 1989, so all in all, he was off to a nice start. We exchanged greetings with a hug and sat in a booth close to the bar.

"So how did voting go?" I asked.

"Good, no long lines, people were kind, and I was in and out, if you know what I mean, hee-hee."

He was corny, but whatever, I continued on, "Would you mind me asking how you are leaning this election year?"

"Republican right down the line," he boasted. Strike one, two, and three. He was out. It was time to abort this mission.

Oddly enough, a migraine train tore through my brain halfway through dinner, the left side to be exact. I apologized for the abrupt interruption of the dizzying nature of my better sense. I cautiously excused myself, made my exit, and walked home. "The cool air will help," I said.

This online dating scheme was clearly not working. Truth be told, with Steve's illness, the sex portion of our relationship was the last thing on both our minds. I had gone roughly seven years with no sex. Even masturbation was getting tiresome. Even though I was fat, a big no-no in the gay world, and old, another no-no, I still felt that I had something to give. I was really not a one-night-stand sort of guy because I have to be connected enough to find someone sexy. Do not get me wrong, I have had my share of "walks of shame," I was choosing not to walk that path this time.

In light of that, I was horny. I was craving the touch of another man. I went on Scruff and Grindr, which are dating apps that show you who is looking for a fun time and how far they are away from you. This resembled fun. It was like shopping, only for sex. You could gather a lot of information just by reading someone's profile and looking at the pictures they chose to post. It was easy to spot the ones with a little crazy on their face, but a few sounded like they were normal enough to start a chitchat with. The random "Hey" or "Handsome man" were usually a good ice-breakers. I chatted back and forth with a couple of people.

Well in to my window shopping, I saw a picture that was all smiles. It was warm and rested atop a square jaw that was nestled in a yellow polo shirt with a popped collar. He was very dashing. I took a risk and attempted to start a conversation with the smile. According to his profile he was sixty-five years old, he was a retired special-needs teacher, and an actor. He was married and not looking for a relationship, obviously.

The married thing threw me a bit since Mother had been cheated on by Father. I could still see her pain. However, all I was hoping to find was someone to go out to dinner with or maybe a movie. That was all I was capable of at the moment, if I had been honest with myself.

I took the leap and reached with the go-to opening, "Hey." His response was, "Hey," and we started a dialogue. We chatted back and forth the whole day, and I got to know him a little better. He reiterated to me that he was married, and in no way was he looking to start anything that would bring unhappiness to his wife and family. This I totally understood, and I respected him more for being so matter-of-fact with me.

We decided to meet at the Texas Roadhouse one evening for dinner and a couple of drinks. I was excited, and like the nerd that I am, I arrived early. He walked in the restaurant wearing a light-blue sweater with a popped collar of white. He had on cargo shorts and cool flip-flops. He looked directly at me and smiled; it was him. We sat at the end of the bar and ordered a round of Makers Mark, double. *I simply adore bourbon, it is always such a nice treat.* We drank, we talked, we ate, we talked, we ordered another round and talked some more. Our knees brushed together several times, and then we decided to touch knees a little more aggressively. We snuck in a few inappropriate gropes here and there. My stomach was doing somersaults with arousal. I learned he was an actor and had quite a successful career. He shared the funniest and most touching story about himself that I will share with you later.

We had finished eating and drinking. Then he asked me if I would like some cherry pie.

"I don't think they have cherry pie here, only apple, cheesecake and some brownie mess," I said.

"No, I have some cherry pie at home. I made it last night."

And he cooks too? I wondered if he did windows.

"Oh," I said, getting his intentions last minute.

"Okay, but I have to take something home for Vic." At the time, Victoria from the internet radio show was staying with me for a while. She had recently ended a relationship, and I was on her support staff for this one.

One order of chicken fingers and fries later, we headed home to deliver the meal. I was excited for Vic to meet the mystery man whose name was James.

Again, Jim was very forthcoming. He told Vic that he was married and was just looking for a new guy friend to hang around with. Maybe a little too much information for a first meeting, but still all good.

We hopped back in his convertible and headed to his place a mere fifteen minutes from me. We parked in the garage to avoid the nosy neighbors that would ask, "So, who was that guy with James in the car?" It was very clandestine in a way.

He ushered me from the garage to his home and on inside. He made his way to the refrigerator, opened it, and presented the cherry pie proudly on the marble countertop. Then, totally by surprise, he kissed me like I have never been kissed before. I had never before experienced a soul connection so sincere in a kiss.

Then things really got hot, quickly. We spent the night doing what we did, in the kitchen, in the dining room, in the living room, and in the bathroom. I think we spent at least an hour in the bathroom exhausting what was possible in the realm of shower sex.

We moved to his bedroom and continued our exploration. It felt like a dance, a very dirty dance. Around 3:00 a.m., we decided to take a break and treat ourselves with a cigarette and a glass of cabernet. We stepped outside onto a three-tiered deck that lead to a huge water feature against the fence.

It was lightly misting, and the full moon made it look like a fantasy destination. We talked, drank, smoked, and laughed. I was clad only in my unbuttoned shirt.

"I really think you're a fascinating guy and handsome and smart, but you could really lose some of that belly," he proffered. I would normally succumb to anger if I ever heard those words, then fire off a similar cutting remark. With him, I just laughed. There was no denying my belly; I worked very hard at creating this new fatness.

"The Girl from Ipanema" was playing quietly in the background. He grabbed my hand and pulled me into a dance hold. We danced by the light of pale moonlight. As we fumbled around, I was secretly freeze framing every movement so I would never forget this time, this movie moment.

The elements stepped in to remind us that it was cold and rainy. We took our glasses in to refill them and headed back upstairs to his bedroom. No lights, just the glow of the moon through the lace-draped windows. I traced every inch of his face with my fingertips once we had retired. We talked some more, laughed some more, and drank each other in, allowing time to stand still. We fell asleep in each other's arms.

I awoke to the sound and smell of coffee brewing. I rolled out of bed, hit the bathroom, did my duty, washed my face, brushed my teeth, and made the bed. I then pulled my clothes on and headed downstairs.

There he was, furnishing us with clean cups, evaporated milk, and Equal, placing them next to the cherry pie that was left out all night, while sporting a semi that poked through his opened robe. I was eager to go again.

"Let's go out for breakfast," he suggested.

"Sure, where do you want to go?" I asked.

"Let's just put the top down and go for a ride. Who knows where we'll end up."

He backed out of the garage and put the top down while I waited out of sight. I quickly jumped in the passenger seat and slid down. Once we were safely out of sight, I sat up and appreciated the wind through my hair. The sun on my face as we drove down Highway 95 doing ninety-five miles an hour. Jim loved to drive and was proud of his lead foot.

We found this weird yet charming, little restaurant in old New Castle. A historic town right on the Delaware River. It's filled with historic buildings with little placards telling you who lived there at one time. Some of these houses were built in the 1700s. William Penn and George Washington made old New Castle their home at one time or another, said history. Now it was filled with antique stores and quaint little restaurants that played host to many new musical artists. It's all very charming.

There was never a break in the conversation with Jim. We both could talk, yet we both listened and heard each other. We finished our eggs Benedict and got back in the convertible for another ride.

"Let's take the long way back," he suggested.

"Fine by me." Let's ride.

We left and headed for nowhere. Jim found some back road, and we followed it not knowing where it led. It was exciting, invigorating, stimulating, and totally out of my comfort zone. I'm more of a I-have-to-go-here-to-get-this-then-return-home kind of guy.

The top was down, the sun was warm, the sky was clear, and we listened to NPR. I was in heaven. There was a show on about the history of the wonderful George and Ira Gershwin. Did I mention I love Broadway? The instrumental version of "Summertime" came on, and Jim started to sing. I turned my head in shock and awe. Here I was, riding in a convertible with the morning spring sun dancing on my face, sitting next to an attractive man who is singing to me. Another movie moment was mentally stored.

Then reality reared its ugly head. I knew I was being dropped off, and he would go back to his wife and his life. I was an adult and knew the parameters. I was prepared to never see Jim again. In my mind, this was the best one night stand I had ever had. I composed myself as we rounded the corner to my street. We kissed and agreed that we both had a good time, and with no mention of another possible meeting. I walked on the wooden pathway to my front door and waved as he drove away.

*I never had that piece of cherry pie.*

Once inside, I was greeted by Victoria. She was waiting patiently to hear of the events of the night. I flopped down on the sofa. Vic sat on the end of the chaise, her hands holding her head up. I spilled my guts or what was left of them. I felt drained yet full. I felt like what I imagined and engine must feel like after an oil change. There was a change and that change was within me. I recalled the adventure I had, skipped some of the more dirty details, but conveyed my state. I have always heard the words *swoon, getting the vapors, smitten,* and *swept off my feet,* but describing them from my own perspective was a new experience.

I now understood those words. I did swoon, but I did not faint. I was smitten. I was swept off my feet, and I did get the vapors. Reality needed to be sidelined for a while because I wanted to relish all these feelings, if only for a short time. I took to my bed and instantly fell asleep, knowing that these feelings actually existed. The fact that I had just experienced these feelings firsthand was dreamlike. I now truly understand what a state of bliss was.

The next day, with coffee in hand and Vic still sleeping, I took my iPad and headed to the balcony. I had left the pool fountain running all night and was delighted to have some quiet time with its soothing sound surrounding me. I logged on to Grindr with the hope that James was online.

He was, and I thanked him for a great evening, trying to sound cool in a suave manner via messenger. I wanted to act aloof but could not. I had a few things to do, as did he. So, we shared idle chitchat throughout the day. Then, while scrolling I landed on a picture of just legs and feet. Hairy man legs do something for me, do not judge me. I chatted with feet man and learned that he was having a little orgy at 5:00 p.m. in his apartment. Feeling more confident now, I was intrigued. I messaged Jim the details and asked if he was interested. We could go together and bail each other out if things should get freaky. I'm no stranger to group sex, but it was usually with people I know.

Jim was game. He had to pop in the shower, and then he would pick me up for our little soiree.

He picked me up, we headed out, we got lost, we found our way, and finally arrived at the door leading to a den of iniquity. We were instructed to open the door, walk in, and head to the bedroom at the end of the hall. We pulled up to the apartment, share a quick joint, for extra confidence and headed in.

The apartment was dark. We made our presence known with a, "Hello, we're here."

"We're down at the end of the hall," an unknown voice called out.

Upon entry to the bedroom at the end of the hall, we walked in on a very hefty older man, nude, and fingering the ass of a younger man in his mid-twenties who was also nude. Jim and I look at each other and started to disrobe.

There was fumbling around, people touching things on other people, open mouths, lube, poppers, groping, probing, a couple spurts, and we were all done. We all cleaned up, exchanged handshakes, and we headed back to the SAAB.

"Well, that was interesting," Jim stated.

"Let's get a drink," I recommend.

We sat the bar in Stewart's, it was a local micro-brewery, we regaled and laughed at what we just experienced. I mean, who the hell did we think we were, rock stars or something?

We talked and talked and talked. I found myself hanging on his every word. He would also flip into speaking Italian, which is a panty dropper for sure. As I listened closer, although not fluent in Italian, I could discern that he was speaking gibberish Italian. I did not care.

Later, we found out that the host of our little whatever-it-was, was a Roman-Catholic priest who lead a very large congregation in a nearby parish. He hosted these little events twice a month. *Do priests pay taxes?*

Throughout the month of May, we saw each other frequently. He got away when he could. Some visits were simply a walk-in, make out, then heavily make out, and he would leave. Time elapsed, fifteen minutes. Some were lengthier, of course. I was taking what I could get.

I acknowledged the guilt of knowing what I was doing. I was playing with another woman's husband. I did not want to be a home wrecker, but I couldn't get enough of him. At night I fashioned pillows in the shape of his body and would hold it tight as I drifted off to dreams of him one day being mine. It was a completely irrational thought process. He made it abundantly clear that he would never leave his wife. I would shake my head to rid myself of the thought, but it lay deep in my mind and in my heart.

One day, Jim had gone see his daughter. She had special needs and lived in a home an hour and a half away. I would not see or hear from him that day.

I logged on to Grindr to see if he was on, but he was not. In his absence, I loaded all the messages we had exchanged and read them again. Honestly, my true calling was in hair, but I've always wanted to be able to call myself a writer. I had been writing a book for seven years, but in my mind, I could not see the ending through. And upon rereading my past work, I realized it was really depressing. So I had shelved that project long ago, but as I was reading, I discovered that I had my next book. All the dirty, filthy, salacious words magically wove themselves into a touching and loving blanket of romance.

I sat down at the computer and started writing immediately. I took all the texts we had shared, word for word, and added my touch to what was being exchanged in the dialogue and how it affected me. I wrote and wrote and wrote. The words were easy to find. I accredited it to the ease and the overall message, of the two people finally finding comfort in their own skins.

I finished that book in a week. Two hundred pages of the intimate conversations between a married man looking for some man-love and a lonely widower trying to move forward after the death of his lover. I called it, *Him and Me: The Text Book Romance of Him and Me,* still available on Amazon.com and Kindle friendly. I gave the first copy of the manuscript to Jim since he had rights of first refusal.

In the first pass of the book, I kept the names, but dropped the last names for legal reasons. Jim came back to me and expressed that he enjoyed the book but asked that I change all the names. I gladly complied and re-submitted the work to Jim. I explained that I would self-publish this book and it would be available for purchase in a few days. He was in agreement, so I went on to publish.

I must have read that book fifty times, combing every detail to ensure a work that I would be proud of always. It was quite a departure from who I was, but the experiences I now possessed altered my understanding and pushed me out of the rut I was in. I was now able to allow another into my life, and I had someone in my life that was genuinely listening to me. Sure, the other men I shared time with listened, but Jim was the first one to truly hear me, and accept me for who I was, without intention of changing me to suit him. It was refreshing.

In an effort to help me make more money, Jim introduced me to a product called Nerium. It was an anti-aging cream that helped one to restore their skin and age backward. Jim's niece was one of the top sellers, and she was recruiting salespeople. The company claimed it was not an MLM or a pyramid-scheme. This was called "direct level marketing." Much like the Faberge Organic shampoo commercial with the tag line, "I told two friends, and she told two friends and so on and so on." Although I wasn't drinking the Kool-Aid just yet, Jim put up the $500 buy-in fee, and I started walking the streets of the internet to peddle my wares. Honestly, the product did and does work. One of the suggestions was to attack your consumer base on Facebook and post twice a day. In turn, some other Nerium acolyte would comment on your post to keep it current in the Facebook feed.

I followed instructions, got some nibbles, but mostly lost a lot of friends because of my endless postings about the product was irritating. Hell, it irritated me. I did have marginal success with it, but having been in the corporate beauty business, I felt this was basically Avon. I grew increasingly disinterested with the game of it.

I had finished the book and posted it for sale on my social media sites. The book was selling, and I was happy. I was surprised by who was buying it. Amazon clued me in on and even gave me a breakdown of who is buying my book. The would provide what age they were, where they lived, and even told you the median income for said areas. The people buying my book were mostly women between the ages of thirty (which makes sense) to seventy-five (that surprised me). The reviews were good, and my readers could see the love story that served as a foundation to hold up the filth Jim and I had experienced.

I was happy with the sales information and looked forward to promoting my book on the radio to direct traffic and increase the interest.

This was when things backfired. Jim's niece, in a show of support, bought and read the book. She then shared it with her mother, Jim's wife's sister. Long story short, between the niece and her mother, they surmised that my book was not a work of fiction, but a detailed account of Jim's indiscretions and my active participation there-in.

Naturally, Jim's wife received a phone call from her sister and purchased the book. The fan was running, shit was going to be everywhere.

The jig was up, our goose was cooked, and our reputations were shot. *Wake up, little Susie*, Jim's wife was furious. My reminder that the book was a work of fiction fell on deaf ears. These were not daft people, and they could see the writing on the wall. We had to cool it off for a while, which killed me inside. I knew that I had opened Pandora's box, and I could not put the calamity back inside. The word *divorce* was mentioned more and more each day.

I did not know what to feel. I felt for his wife, to learn after forty-three years of marriage that your husband is stepping out with another *man*? Devastation, shame, fear, uncertainty, guilt, embarrassment were only a few emotions that I could imagine her visiting.

It was a sunny Sunday afternoon when I received a text from Jim saying that he wanted to stop by and share some information. We sat outside, sipping on vino, as he told me that we could no longer continue seeing each other. His wife was adamant that Jim was to stop seeing me immediately. This was extremely unsettling for me for many reasons. I had grown to love this man. I admired him for who he was, what he did, what he does, and how he treated me. I listened and agreed to his terms in the hope of one day, he would step out of the proverbial closet and be himself.

We did the no-talking, no-communication thing for two days. Frustrated, I emailed him with a single statement that said, "This sucks." Within minutes I received a response with a link to Jon McLaughlin's song, "Doesn't Mean Good-bye." *If you have never listened to it, I would highly recommend you look it up on YouTube.* No one had ever sent me a song, and the words were so poignant that I was moved to crocodile-sized tears. This was surprising to me as I didn't know crocodiles cried. All kidding aside, it moved me. He was with his wife in Florida during this time, and his absence was not only felt, it was an ache that I wasn't familiar with. Their trip to Florida was intended for Jim and his wife to reconnect. This was a fair request on her part after the middle-of-the-night call I received from her.

I was listening over a show that Vic and I recently finished. It was a Thursday night show, and I spent most of the evening calling the guests back and thanking them for their time spent with us. The phone rang, and I was certain it was another friend, most noted for her middle-of-the-night drunken rants. I had nothing to do but listen to myself so I answered the phone. Much to my dismay, the voice was that of Jim's wife.

"Hi Michael. Jim's wife here."

I checked the clock. It was 4:10 a.m. My stomach fell out of my ass. I could not run. I could not hide. I calmly listened to her as she recalled several loving moments in their forty-three years of marriage. I listened to what she endured with regard to the loss of their two other children who had passed away. I listened to her explain the love they shared for their only living daughter who was thirty-six at the time, living with special needs in a caring group home. I listened and I heard her. It was actually more of pleasant call than I had expected. At the end of the conversation, she asked if she could ask me a favor. "Will you just stop seeing my husband," was her request.

I took a moment, paused, and replied, "No, I can't do that. Plus, it's not just up to me." I meant her no disrespect, I was simply being honest with my reply.

Little did I know, Jim was listening to her talk to me while standing literally in the shadows at the foot of the stairs.

The next day, I told Jim of the call. He was more than familiar and simply apologized on her behalf. In my eyes, there was nothing to apologize for in my mind. I would have done the same thing if I were in her shoes. I am not sure if I could have been as polite as she was, but, nonetheless, I will, I have, and I would fight for my man.

The couple's reconnection failed, and Jim's divorce was on the table, negotiations were underway. Jim forfeited the house, the new SAAB, agreed to her terms, agreed to her conditions, and took a bath, so to speak.

The silver lining in this clouded storm was that Jim was now on the path to his own understanding, and we were still seeing each other, now with more frequency.

With the quest to keep my financial head above water, I took in a boarder from Canada whose specialty was customizing the interiors of privately purchased planes. I found this fascinating. He was a good roommate, low maintenance, easygoing. He kept odd working hours, and I did not mind. I enjoyed having someone around who loved yard work, a chore I detest to this day. He even took it upon himself to organize a yard cleaning crew to clean out the side of the backyard that I still purposely choose to ignore. He paid the rent on time, and, all in all, he was a good guy.

Picture the scene here … it was a lazy Friday night. The temperature was in the high 80s. All the windows were open allowing the heavy summer air to fill the house with the scent of fresh cut grass. Jim and I are on the outdoor sofa, sharing a toke, and some good vino. We are laughing and genuinely enjoying life. It was around 8:00 p.m.

All of a sudden, two people ran in from the left of the deck, two people entered from the right of the deck, and someone comes through the front door to meet his pals. All are clad in black, faces covered, eyes poking out through the slits in their masks. Guns are pulled and thrust in our face. It all happened so fast that I really did not comprehend the intensity of the goings-on. "Get up," was the instruction.

Still not understanding the gravity of what was happening, I received a knock to the head with a gun.

"Move!" We stood up and were ushered into the piano room. Jim and I were clad only in our Speedos. Jim's friend was in from Los

Angeles, Garrett. He was resting in the guest room. They threw the three of us down on the floor in the piano room. They restrained us with zip-ties at the hands and feet. Then, a blanket was thrown over our heads. That's when panic set in for me.

They wanted to know where the money and the drugs were. Sure, I had money in the house, but all I had was the end of a bag of pot in the drug department. These kids were robbing the wrong house. Garrett starts to freak out and shouts, "Michael, just tell them where the money is." That was helpful. I got a couple extra knocks to the head with the butt of another gun, and I offered up the cash. We heard them going through everything, knocking things on the floor.

"What the hell is that smell?" One of the intruders asked his hostages.

"Look, I shit myself," I explained.

"Why?" He questioned me directly now. "Dude, this is some really serious shit going on," I replied.

Jim and I were laying on the floor no more than two inches away from each other. Jim was maintaining his composure much better than I was at the moment. He was an actor, he had done this scene several times, was my only rationalization. "Just breathe with me," he said calmingly. We matched our breathing patterns and he calmed me down, even as the assailants were dripping hot candle wax down my hairy, Speedo-clad legs. *What was that all about, seriously?*

I heard a door open. It was my downstairs boarder. The intruders left us and headed downstairs to address the newcomer. We listened as they beat the shit out of him. Garrett took the initiative in the turn of events and was able to break free of his ties. He exited through a bedroom patio access door and jumped the fence, triggering the alarm from a lookout, who was standing in the driveway. Garrett ran to the gas station across the street and called the police.

"We gotta go," called the outdoor lookout. We heard a scramble, then all was silent. Jim and I did not know what to do. My downstairs boarder ran up the stairs, grabbed a knife from the kitchen, and he cut us free. Jim and I got up and watched as the gang steals the boarder's car, filled with his airplane customization work tools. They were gone. The whole episode, including the shitting of my Speedo, lasted approximately ten minutes. In hindsight, it seemed like an eternity.

I looked around the house. Every cupboard and every drawer was emptied on the floor. The living room furniture was tipped over. The bedrooms were ransacked. Truly a sight that one would think to see during an episode of *CSI*. Bewildered, confused, and shocked, we called the police and awaited their arrival.

Around thirty cops arrived at our crime scene. All were making sure not to ruffle the disarray while they collected the needed clues and evidence to catch the unwelcomed visitors. Jim, Garrett, and I were escorted to the cop shop and waited endlessly as the investigator on shift went over our statements. We left the police station around 4:00 a.m. and went back to Jim's house. We drank more wine and rehashed the events of the previous evening. I don't think anyone slept more than an hour before we headed back to my house to assess the damage. We walked in and were greeted by an officer that stayed all night to watch over the broken house.

We relieved him from his post and kicked papers around to make our way to the dining room. Everything, everywhere!

I had to cancel all my credit cards; they had stolen my wallet, and they had made off with roughly three thousand dollars in cash. They were kind enough to leave my passport behind, however.

In the trashed kitchen, I noticed a glass used to drink the last of the wine Jim and I opened the night before. They had also helped themselves to some cookies. I guess home invasion can make you hungry. More police arrived to take one last look around, and I informed them of the missing items and potential clues.

It took the three of us three hours to restore the house to its original glory. I have heard others explain the feeling of being violated after a robbery on news reports, and I now understood that feeling. Knowing that someone touched my underwear repulsed me. They had even gone through the drawer where I kept a few dildos, and I was silently relieved that they chose not to torture us with aggressive anal penetration. Sometimes fantasies should remain as a fantasy, better to keep that in the mind.

The thieves were the same people that cleaned out the side of my yard the week prior. They were part of a ring that were traveling all over Delaware and Pennsylvania. Their last heist was an elderly couple who owned a jewelry business. The wife was shot in the head, execution style, and her husband was shot in the back as he ran for his life. We were unscathed, except for the memory. The home invasion experience messed with my mind as much as the details of the assailants. For months, I was skittish, hyper-aware of my surroundings, and had trouble sleeping. During this time, Jim's divorce was settled, and he moved in with me.

Today, life with James is more than a delight. I now have a reason to wake up. I am not yelled at. No one hits me. No one demeans me. No one thinks my ideas are stupid. I only feel love and understanding. We will still spend an entire evening talking and trying to solve and understand the ways of the world. My life now is calm and filled with love every day.

I would like to say that I am lucky to have found someone who makes me feel as good as I do, but that would be wrong. It was the path and the decisions I made along the way, that led me to Jim. I understand, now, that I deserve to feel good. I deserve to feel wanted, loved, respected, and acknowledged. I get to be me, which is a continual work in progress.

I do believe that we are all intrinsically the same. Color, race, preference, gender, and beliefs all contribute to the human race fabric. When we are happy with who we are, there is a tender calmness that washes over the soul. When you accept who you are, or in my case, when you have someone next to you who means no harm, but is willing to help you become your authentic self, that I call utopia.

Imagine there's no heaven.
It's easy if you try.
No hell below us
Above us only sky.

The truth of the matter is, after considering all that I have endured, I am a survivor. With all the learning and information I now hold, I am still the seven-year-old boy inside. I think we all are like that. We are all just old children, forever seeking love, understanding, and comfort. As an individual, I continually monitor my thoughts, my ego, my judgments, my expectations, and I'm still working on removing fear. That's a hard one for me.

The eternal quest for understanding one's self is the quintessential carrot that some of us choose to focus on. It is like exercise. It requires daily, sometimes hourly, attention.

I choose to believe, and continue to believe, that all of us, at one time or another, have good intentions. Sometimes the path some take can be violent, fear based, and irrational, but the ends somehow justify the means.

We are all trying.

Keep trying. It's worth it, but that's just my two cents.

Carry on.

Live long and prosper, but only if you choose to do so.

# Manifestation

As this book comes to print, I continue to live, laugh, and learn with Jim. This book is now on the New York Times Best Seller List for three weeks now. Both Jim and I are thrilled that these words are being read and may be influential to some.

Stephanie and Michael Knight have become our new best friends. We could not have done this book without their brilliant editing. Their active consideration and participation on this book is nothing short of stellar, and I cannot sing their praises loud enough.

Life with Jim continues to be a wonderful ride. I picked well this time. We grow together and encourage each other in every way possible. I still get butterflies in my stomach when I see him. We have a note on the fridge that says, "What can I do to make my day better? What can I do to make your day better?" I read it every day. I apply that every day. Even if it is anticipating when I think he would like a cup of tea, small effort is noted and appreciated. He does the same for me. We live in a wonderfully functional house, tastefully decorated and modestly enjoyed. Any anger is confronted and diffused during the moment. Nothing festers within. It's a nice change.

This book will be made into a movie and go on to win the Oscar for best film, best screenplay, best editing, and best actor and actress in a motion picture. Jim and I will wear tuxedos and graciously meet those who watched and enjoyed. We will attend a few parties, then head to In-and-Out to get two doubles and share an order of well-done fries. Exhausted and exhilarated, we take the company limo back to our deluxe suite at the Beverly Hills Hotel. We will pour our last bourbon for the evening, turn on CNN, and I will check my email, flooded with congratulatory messages from people I do not know, and people who I have always wanted to know. We will finish our Knob Creeks and retire to the king-sized bed wrapped in 1,300-thread count Egyptian cotton sheets.

I will close my eyes and wonder, *Could this get any better?*
We will see.
Sleep.

# About the Author

THIS CANADIAN-BORN, PRAIRIE-BORN BOY STARTED by working at his parents restaurant at the age of seven. Realizing he was a little different from the other boys, he left his small town following a hunch that things were different than he could ever imagine. He spent twenty-five years in the beauty industry, moved into film, theater, and television doing what he could to challenge his interpersonal growth. His radio show, heard in over thirty-five countries, featured the attempt to unite those also on the path of greater understanding. *Through the Fire*, his latest work is followed by *Reflections from the Throne: Universal Thinking during Your Daily Constitutional*, and *A Story: The Textbook Romance of Him and Me*. He also thinks he's a singer at times.